OUT OF AFRICA:

THE BREAKAWAY ANGLICAN CHURCHES

A Movement With a Mission

Ross Lindsay

Forewords by Emmanuel Kolini and David Virtue

Out of Africa: The Breakaway Anglican Churches
A Movement with a Mission
by Ross Lindsay

Printed in the United States of America

ISBN 9781613796054

www.xulonpress.com

CONTENTS

DEDICATION

This book is dedicated to:

Emmanuel Kolini, Archbishop of Rwanda (retired)

John Rucyahana, Bishop of the Shyria Diocese, Rwanda (retired)

Moses Tay, Archbishop of South East Asia (retired)

Bishop FitzSimmons Allison, Bishop of South Carolina (retired)

Bishop Alex D. Dickson, Bishop of West Tennessee (retired)

Professor Norman C. Doe, the Director of the Centre of Law and Religion at Cardiff University Law School, Cardiff, Wales

The Rev. Canon Dr. Kevin F. Donlon, the Canon for Ecclesiastical Affairs, Anglican Mission in the Americas, Tampa, Florida

FOREWORD
BY DAVID VIRTUE

For nearly 40 years, leaders in The Episcopal Church (TEC) have endeavored to dumb down and override Holy Scripture with innovative doctrines, and rewrite church history. They have succeeded beyond their wildest dreams, perhaps even those of Friedrich Schleiermacher, the "Father of Modern Protestant Theology." In their ruthless pursuit of power, leaders within The Episcopal Church have deposed bishops and priests, forced a crisis of conscience on whole dioceses, and demanded an allegiance to "strange and erroneous doctrines" that have imperiled their souls and those that they serve.

Now, it is all becoming unraveled. The Episcopal Church's growth from the 19th Century to the mid 20th Century was significant, but in the last 30 years it has been all downhill. The price for the heresies of Bishop John Shelby Spong and his fellow revisionist bishops along with the church's subsequent sexual innovations has been significant, spiritually crippling, and deadly.

The first shot fired in the "theological wars" between the revisionist bishops of TEC and the orthodox Archbishops of the Anglican Communion came from All Saints Church in Pawleys Island, South Carolina.

It resulted in the consecrations of two godly men in Singapore – Chuck Murphy and John Rodgers—as missionary bishops *to* the United States and Canada. That action not only shook up The Episcopal Church and its Presiding Bishop, but also the Archbishop of Canterbury and, in time, the wider Anglican Communion. It forced a realignment that continues to this day.

No one conceived that a small hamlet of 10,000 souls in coastal South Carolina would be the birthplace of an ecclesiastical and spiritual revolution that would rock the world of 70 million Anglicans, but that is precisely what happened.

In this book, Ross Lindsay, the Chancellor of All Saints Church and an astute canon lawyer, tells the story of those early years as the leaders at All Saints Church struggled over whether or not to remain within The Episcopal Church. In the end, they walked away. As a result, the Anglican Mission in the Americas was born as a missionary outreach of the Anglican Church of Rwanda—a movement with a mission to reach the 130 million unchurched Americans.

The price for abandoning The Episcopal Church has been high. Lawsuits over its church property continued for more than a decade. At the same time, however, a whole new movement emerged—The Anglican Mission, that has continued to grow, planting an average of one new Anglican congregation every three weeks. And a new theologically conservative church for Anglicans in North America—the Anglican Church of North America (ACNA). Today this new face of Anglicanism claims more than 100,000 souls in nearly 1,000 churches across North America. A decade ago, no one would have believed it possible.

This book traces in detail, with timelines, the players that made it all happen—the emergence of the breakaway Anglican churches and their transformation into a new religious movement and a new church of faithful Anglicans. These breakaway Anglican churches will, for a time, be seen as schismatic, but as they grow stronger, they will take their place among the pantheon of global Anglican leaders. They will be seen as the bearers of the true flame of Anglicanism in North America. Time is on their side.

David W. Virtue DD
VIRTUEONLINE
West Chester, PA
June 2011

FOREWORD
BY EMMANUEL KOLINI

The final days of the 20th Century and the beginning of the 21st Century will prove to be monumental in history when one considers the changes that occurred politically, socially, and economically throughout the globe. The same is true in the world of faith and religion, and in particular, in Anglicanism. These days are well documented by Dr. Ross Lindsay in this hallmark book.

Lindsay chronicles well the realignment of Anglicanism that was birthed at All Saints Church in Pawleys Island, South Carolina as a direct result of the failings at Lambeth Conference 1998. As the realignment has taken shape, the Anglican Church of Rwanda and the Anglican Mission in the Americas have blazed a trail that was rooted in the ancient missionary movements of the Celtic Church.

The House of Bishops in Rwanda, along with Bishops Chuck Murphy and John Rodgers, grasped fully the need for a realigned Anglicanism that embraced what we now know as the Three Streams: the catholic revival movement, the charismatic renewal movement, and the evangelical movement. Each has significant graces and blessings that they offer to the Anglican celebration of the Gospel while being rooted in the "common historic faith once delivered to the saints."

The Province of Rwanda and the Anglican Mission heralded the dawning of a new day in Anglicanism. The coming together of Global South Primates from various levels of churchmanship has provided a renewed impetus for cooperation and collaboration in mission and ministry among evangelicals, charismatics, and catholics. The Global South Task Forces on theological education and formation, the missionary outreaches through the Anglican Mission in the Americas (Anglican Mission), the Convocation of Anglican Churches in North America (CANA), and cooperative efforts between them and the Anglican Church of North America (ACNA), all serve as strong indicators that such a coming together is fortuitous and God's will. Ross Lindsay has profiled well the journey and these movements in the Anglican realignment that have emerged in North America and in the Global South.

Numerous voices, from Archbishop Akinola to the newly elected Archbishop of Rwanda, Onesphore Rawje, have stressed that the call of the three orthodox streams of Anglicanism is to mission. Few would quibble with the primacy of this vocation, but it assumes that there is agreement on the nature of mission within the three streams. Ross Lindsay reminds us that missiology and ecclesiology go hand in hand. While all would agree that mission is derived from the Scriptures, the instruments to apply that sacred message for each of these three streams is the challenge ahead of us.

The Anglican Mission has endeavored to confront the moral, political, and social influences of secularism. If the mission of the church is to preach the Word correctly and to rightly administer the sacraments as part of this mission, then the question of mission and ecclesiology must be addressed as Ross Lindsay points out in this astute overview.

The benefits of conciliar ecclesiology have been discussed recently, and I am pleased that the Anglican Church of Rwanda and the Anglican Mission have been voices in this conversation. As the Rwandan bishops noted at the All African Bishops Conference in Kampala 2010, conciliar ecclesiology can offer a renewed way of perceiving the relationship between Anglicanism and the world. Thank you Ross Lindsay for underscoring our call to both missiology and conciliar ecclesiology in this book.

The Most Reverend Emmanuel Musaba Kolini
Archbishop of Rwanda (retired)
Pentecost 2011

AUTHOR'S PREFACE

I have had the privilege of worshiping at All Saints Church in Pawleys Island, South Carolina for almost 30 years, and I have witnessed first-hand the transformation of a small colonial congregation with less than 80 attendees into an internationally recognized congregation with over 800 in average Sunday attendance. However, there is much more to the All Saints Church story than its remarkable growth and transformation. An entire movement grew out of this congregation, the breakaway Anglican churches and the Anglican Mission in the Americas (The Anglican Mission). The headquarters for The Anglican Mission was located on the campus of All Saints Church for ten years and is still located in Pawleys Island.

I turned fifty in 2000, the same year that Chuck Murphy, the twentieth rector of All Saints Church, was consecrated in Singapore as a "missionary bishop" *to* the United States. Someone gave me Bob Buford's book, *Half-Time,* for my birthday, from which I learned that I was entering my "second-half" and that "significance" was a more desirable goal than "success" during my second half.

So, I immediately sought the advice and counsel of my pastor, friend, and mentor, Chuck Murphy, as to what "significant" things that I might accomplish for my Lord and for All Saints Church during my second-half. Chuck Murphy suggested that I first improve my "head-knowledge" of the Scriptures by attending the Institute of Christian Leadership that was located on the campus of All Saints Church. Philip Comfort, the Dean of the Institute, then encouraged me to pursue a Ph.D. in Theology at London School of Theology. The Institute needed another Ph.D. in order to become a fully accredited satellite campus for Trinity School for Ministry in Pittsburgh and Columbia Biblical Seminary and School for Missions in Columbia, South Carolina.

During the first week of my studies at the Institute, Ed Salmon, the Episcopal Bishop of the Diocese of South Carolina, filed a "legal notice" in the Georgetown County Courthouse stating that all of the property owned and used by All Saints Church for over 250 years was held "in trust for The Episcopal Church and the Episcopal Diocese of South Carolina." I was a tax attorney, not a real estate attorney nor a canon lawyer. However, the Vestry of All Saints Church retained me for the sum of one dollar per year to serve as the church's Chancellor for the sole purpose of retaining and overseeing a team of litigators who fought diligently for the next ten years to retain the 60 acre campus of All Saints Church.

I soon realized that church law involved much more than civil real estate and corporate law. It also involved "canon law," an obtuse collection of constitutions and "canons" that were first codified in the 12th century. So, while I was in London pursuing my Ph.D., I also enrolled in the Centre for Law and Religion at Cardiff University Law School in Cardiff, Wales as a candidate for a Master of Laws (L.L.M.) in Canon Law. While studying in Cardiff, I met my good friend, Kevin Donlon of Tampa, Florida, an Oxford trained church historian and an astute canon lawyer.

With the knowledge that I had gained at Cardiff Law School, I was able to testify in the All Saints Church property trial in 2007 that The Episcopal Church ("TEC") had no "canons" that related to real property when All Saints Church acquired its 60 acre campus. In 2009, the South Carolina Supreme Court agreed and ruled in favor of All Saints Church, and the local congregation was allowed to retain all 60 acres of its property and its name, which was another hotly contested issue in the lawsuit.

If my efforts as Chancellor of All Saints Church and my testimony at the All Saints Church property trial contributed something "significant" to the mission and ministry of All Saints Church, to God be the Glory. However, any contribution that I made paled in comparison to that of Chuck Murphy, T.J. Johnston, Thad Barnum, Jon Shuler, Bishop John Rucyahana, Archbishop Emmanuel Kolini of Rwanda and many other bold men who dared to contravene almost 2,000 years of canon law and tradition in order to begin the breakaway Anglican church movement.

These Godly men not only preserved and protected the congregation of All Saints Church. With God's help, they began a new religious movement that has helped spread the Gospel throughout the United States and into Canada and has preserved Anglicanism in North America in the process. Thanks be to God for these soldiers of Christ.

This story needed to be told. Telling it has been a daunting task. May it be read by generations to come so that they will know how far we have come, but also recognize how far we have to go.

Ross M. Lindsay, III "Buddy"
Pawleys Island, South Carolina
June 2011

1

INTRODUCTION

OUT OF AFRICA:
THE NEXT CHRISTENDOM

On January 29, 2000, in Singapore, the Anglican Archbishops of Rwanda (Africa) and South East Asia contravened almost 2,000 years of canon law (church law) and tradition by consecrating two American Episcopal priests as "Missionary Bishops" *to* the United States and Canada. For centuries, churches in the West had sent missionaries into Africa, Asia, and Latin America. On January 29, 2000, the tables were turned. The West became the "missionfield."

Many questions arose in the days and weeks following the "Singapore Consecrations," and many faithful Anglicans on both sides of the Atlantic asked why the consecrations were necessary. One English Vicar shared the following observations in what quickly became an endless debate of the issue on the Internet:

For thirty years now, enthusiasts for the liberal agenda [in The Episcopal Church (TEC)] have claimed an implausible blend of spiritual inspiration and secular common sense to lead in ways plainly contrary to the Word of God. They have achieved this by a ruthless quest for power, the hijacking of institutions, the deliberate and wholesale deposition of orthodox priests, and piecemeal by the claim of Provincial Autonomy. . . . Singapore, right or wrong, has sent a strong warning shot across the bows of the liberal bark.

The Next Christendom

In *The Next Christendom,* Professor Philip Jenkins described what he called the "transformation of religion" worldwide. According to Jenkins, over the past century, the center of gravity in the Christian world has shifted inexorably southward to Africa, Asia, and Latin America; and the Anglican Communion has not been an exception. Jenkins observed:

The Anglican Communion now claims over 70 million members worldwide. [However,] Anglicans in the British Isles are massively outnumbered overseas . . . . Nigeria alone claims 20 million baptized Anglicans . . . . By 2050, the global total of Anglicans will be approaching 150 million, of whom only a tiny minority will be white Europeans.

While, the Church of England can barely muster one million Anglicans on Easter Sunday and Christmas, *The New York Times* reported recently that every week hundreds of thousands of Nigerians sit through hours of exhaust fumes and squealing horns to reach evangelical campgrounds. When they finally arrive, they worship in Anglican churches as large as airplane hangers in worship services that are held at 9 o'clock every Friday night.

The 1998 Lambeth Conference

Every ten years, the Archbishop of Canterbury, the titular head of the worldwide Anglican Communion, invites all Anglican bishops to gather at Lambeth Palace in London. The Lambeth Conference held in 1998 became the "tipping point" for the Anglican Communion theologically, because, for the first time, the delegates from the southern hemisphere (Africa, Asia and Latin America) made their voices heard. Historically, the adage used to describe the Lambeth Conferences had been: "The Americans pay, the Africans pray, and the British draft the resolutions." However, the Africans (and other Primates from the southern hemisphere) did do more than "pray" at the 1998 Lambeth Conference.

The stage was set as 736 bishops from 37 of the 38 provinces of the Anglican Communion traveled to Lambeth Palace for the 13th Lambeth Conference that convened in July 1998. Ten years earlier, at the 1988 Lambeth Conference, women's ordination had been a divisive topic. At Lambeth 1998, the *Eames Commission* that had been created to monitor the issue reported that women's ordination had largely become a "non-issue." However, the delegates at Lambeth 1998 had been forewarned that "homosexuality" would be the dividing issue at this conference.

Of the 736 bishops, who registered at the 1998 Lambeth Conference, only 316 were from the United States, Canada, and Europe; while 224 were from Africa, and 95 were from Asia. The delegates from the southern hemisphere made their presence known. According to the *Church Times,* the delegation from the "Global South" was fully in control during the debate on homosexuality. "By every reckoning," the *Church Times* observed, "it was a pivotal moment in the life of the Anglican Communion." A consortium of bishops from Africa, Asia, and Latin America, who were joined by conservative bishops from the United States, succeeded in having the conference adopt a biblically based statement on human sexuality. The vote was 526 to 70 with 45 abstentions.

Among other things, the statement provided that the Conference, in view of the teaching of Scripture:

Upholds faithfulness in marriage between a man and a woman in lifelong union;

Cannot advise the legitimizing or blessing of same sex unions nor ordaining those involved in same gender unions;

Notes the significance of the Kuala Lumpur Statement on Human Sexuality.

Therefore, the delegates from the Global South had made their presence known. They had also prevailed by having the Lambeth Conference adopt a biblically based resolution dealing with human sexuality, one that specifically acknowledged the significance of their Kuala Lumpur Statement.

Chuck Murphy Convened the First Promise Roundtable in Pawleys Island

In September 1997, Chuck Murphy, the Rector of All Saints, Church in Pawleys, South Carolina called together a broad coalition of orthodox Episcopal leaders whose stated goal was to "preserve the Anglican faith in the United States of America." The members of this coalition, the *First Promise Roundtable,* were united in their submission to the sovereign authority of Holy Scripture, the historic Creeds, the traditional Faith of the Prayer Book, the resolutions of the 1998 Lambeth Conference, the Kuala Lumpur Statement, and the Dallas Statement.

Sixteen months later, Chuck Murphy and John Rodgers were consecrated in Singapore as missionary bishops to the United States and Canada. Following the Singapore consecrations, the tiny coastal hamlet of Pawleys Island, South Carolina was besieged with reporters wanting to interview Chuck Murphy. For a season, Pawleys Island became the epicenter of the theological battles that were beginning to rage within the wider Anglican Communion. "Why did God choose Pawleys Island? Chuck Murphy?" a reporter from the *Wall Street Journal* asked the CEO of The Anglican Mission who replied: "Why did God choose Bethlehem? the Jews?"

This book tells the story of the breakaway Anglican churches and the new religious movement that emerged following the Singapore Consecrations. Before examining the breakaway Anglican churches in detail, Chapter 2 recounts the rise and fall of The Episcopal Church in the United States. Chapter 3 discusses the origin and the nature of religious movements generally and the religious movements that evolved out of The Episcopal Church. Chapter 4 summarizes the robust history of Pawleys Island and All Saints Church, the place where the breakaway Anglican church movement began; and Chapter 5 presents a biographical sketch of Chuck Murphy, the man behind the movement. The remaining chapters examine the political and juridical contexts in which the breakaway Anglican churches emerged.

2

The Rise and Fall of The Episcopal Church

In *The Churching of America*, sociologists Roger Finke and Rodney Stark documented that, during the 18th century, the well-educated and profession-ally trained Anglican clergymen were no match for the energetic and non-professionally trained Baptist and Methodist circuit riders. Nevertheless, The Episcopal Church in the United States (TEC) thrived from 1830 through 1960.

Growth was the Trend in TEC from 1830 through 1960

The data in the table below reveal that TEC grew consistently between 1830 and 1960; however, a fur-ther analysis of the data reveals that the rate of growth for TEC actually peaked in 1880 and again in 1930. In addition, while TEC's "market share" in terms of the total United States population ("market share P"), continued to increase nominally until 1960, TEC's market share in terms of inclusive church membership ("market share M'"), actually peaked in 1910.

At least two factors contributed to the sustained growth of TEC between 1830 and 1960. First, TEC more than doubled its number of parishes between 1880 and 1920 from 4,151 to 8,365. As a result, TEC tripled its number of communicants and increased its market share by over 46 percent. However, between 1920 and 1965, the number of TEC parishes in the United States actually *decreased* by 10 percent.

Sociologists of religion have determined that there is a direct correlation between church growth and decline and the increase or decrease in the number of congregations within a church. Since 1968, the number of TEC congregations has decreased consistently as has its number of communicants.

Second, TEC remained *one church* following the Civil War, unlike the Presbyterian, Methodist, and Baptist churches in the United States, all three of which underwent schismatic divisions into northern and southern bodies as a result of differing views on slavery. Those denominations that were divided lost much of their momentum, while TEC actually gained momentum in the decades following the Civil War. Therefore, *growth* was the trend of TEC from 1830 through 1960.

Episcopal Church Communicants 1830-1960
Rate of Growth and Market Share

Year	Communicants	Rate of Growth	Market Share (M)	Market Share (P)
1830	30,939	n/a	n/a	.24
1840	55,477	79.3%	n/a	.33
1850	89,359	61.1%	n/a	.39
1860	146,588	64.0%	n/a	.47
1870	207,762	41.7%	n/a	.52
1880	345,841	66.5%	n/a	.69
1890	508,292	47.0%	1.21	.81
1900	719,540	41.6%	2.05	.94
1910	946,252	31.5%	2.26	1.03
1920	1,073,832	13.5%	1.97	1.01
1930	1,254,227	16.8%	2.12	1.02
1940	1,449,327	15.6%	2.24	1.09
1950	1,651,426	13.9%	1.90	1.09
1960	2,027,671	22.8%	1.77	1.13

Sources: Data for 1830 through 1920 was taken from *The Episcopal Church Annual: 1966.* Data for 1930 through 1960 was supplied by The Episcopal Church Center, New York, NY.

Although, its rate of growth had begun to decrease decades earlier, the actual number of communicants in TEC did not peak until 1968 at 2,280,077. Since 1968, TEC's number of communicants decreased continually as the following table illustrates.

TEC Communicants, Rates of Change and Market Share from 1968 through 1993

Year	Communicants	Rate of Change	Market Share (M)	Market Share (P)
1968	2,280,077	4.3%	1.78%	1.14%
1973	2,120,482	- 7.0%	1.62%	1.00%
1978	1,981,913	- 6.5%	1.49%	.89%
1983	1,906,618	- 3.8%	1.43%	.81%
1988	1,725,581	- 9.5%	1.19%	.70%
1993	1,641,712	- 4.9%	1.07%	.63%
Total	- 638,365	- 28.0%	- 40.0%	- 44.7%

Sources: K. Hadaway, Director of Research, The Episcopal Church Center, New York, NY; *Yearbook of American & Canadian Churches; United States Census, Statistical Abstract: 2003.*

The preceding table also presents TEC's market share in terms of the total membership in United States churches and in terms of the total population of the United States. With respect to the inclusive membership of churches in the United States, TEC lost 40 percent of its market share between 1968 and 1993; and in terms of the total population, TEC lost almost 45 percent of its market share. The rates of change in the number of communicants varied during each five year period; however, its market share decreased consistently in all periods, both in terms of church membership and in terms of the total population.

A Crisis Develops Within the Largest American Churches

In *The Gathering Storm*, sociologist Jeffrey Hadden described a tumultuous storm that hit the largest American churches during the second half of the twentieth century. According to Hadden, beginning in the mid 1960s, the American churches were presented with a threefold crisis: a crisis of meaning and purpose, a crisis of belief, and a crisis of authority. Hadden predicted accurately that this deep and entangling crisis would seriously disrupt or alter the very nature of the church in the United States.

The table on the next page illustrates the extent of the disruption that occurred in the largest American churches by comparing their growth rates from 1950 through 1975 with their growth rates from 1975 through 2000. Several significant observations can be made from the data. First, between 1950 and 1975, eight of the nine largest churches in the United States had positive rates of growth, and four of the eight had rates of growth that exceeded the rate of growth of the general population.

However, between 1975 and 2000, only four of the largest churches in the United States had positive rates of growth; and only two of those, the Assemblies of God (Pentecostal) and the Church of Jesus Christ of Latter Day Saints (Mormon), grew at a rate that was greater than the rate of growth of the general population. Also, the rate of growth for The Episcopal Church (TEC) decreased dramatically from a positive 24 percent between 1950 and 1975 to a negative 18 percent between 1975 and 2000. In fact, TEC had the greatest rate of decline in number of communicants of the nine largest churches.

Growth Rates of the Largest Churches in the United States

1950-1975		1975-2000	
Southern Baptist	.79	Assemblies of God	2.27
Roman Catholic	.65	Latter Day Saints	1.18
Lutheran-MS	.59	Roman Catholic	.27
Am. Lutheran	.43	Southern Baptist	.24
Episcopal	**.24**	Presbyterian USA	- .01
Evan. Lutheran	.19	Evan. Lutheran	- .04
Presbyterian USA	.14	Lutheran-MS	- .06
United Methodist	.02	United Methodist	- .15
Church of Christ	- .07	**Episcopal**	**- .18**
U.S. Population	.40	U.S. Population	.29

Source: *Yearbook of American & Canadian Churches: 1952, 1977, 2002;*

The crisis that began within The Episcopal Church (TEC) during the 1960s continued unabated into the twenty-first century. For example, in October 2006, C. Kirk Hadaway, the Director of Research for The Episcopal Church, reported that TEC had lost over 122,000 members, or an additional five percent of its total membership, between 2002 and 2005. This latest decline within TEC was fueled by a number of sizeable orthodox parishes that elected to sever their canonical ties to TEC following Gene Robinson's consecration as its first openly gay bishop.

However, long before the Robinson Consecration, groups of theologically conservative bishops and priests within TEC had begun several evangelical renewal movements within the denomination. The next chapter examines two types of religious movements: evangelical renewal movements (ERMs) and new religious movements (NRMs).

3

Evangelical Renewal Movements (ERMs) and New Religious Movements (NRMs)

At the dawn of the 21st century, two interesting features on the American religious landscape began to play a critical role in North American Anglicanism: ERMs (evangelical renewal movements) and NRMs (new religious movements), both of which were a product of resurgent evangelicalism in the United States. ERMs are movements that evolve *within* churches or denominations, while NRMs are movements that evolve *outside* of churches or denominations.

According to sociologists of religion Michael Hamilton and Jennifer McKinney: "Contrary to folk wisdom and traditional sociological theory, the mainline Protestant denominations may be poised for a historic change—a return to orthodox Christianity." Hamilton and McKinney cited a previous study by McKinney and Roger Finke that revealed the following:

Evangelical renewal movements (ERMs) are pro-
liferating within traditional mainline denominations.
The American Baptist Church, Disciples of Christ,
The Episcopal Church, Lutheran Church of America,
Presbyterian Church USA, United Methodist Church,
and the United Church of Christ all have at least one
active movement calling for renewal and a return to
traditional teaching.

Hamilton and McKinney found in their study that
the largest ERMs were in the United Methodist and the
Presbyterian USA churches.

Hamilton and McKinney also observed that, unlike
the revival that occurred in the mainline churches
during the 1950s, the younger clergy were leading
these ERMs. Therefore, they concluded: "If all else
fails, these evangelical insurgents may simply outlive
the liberals."

PCUSA, UMC, and TEC Were Staring Chaos in the Face

In *The Remnant Spirit,* sociologist Douglas Cowan
observed that Christianity often has found itself within
the ebb and flow of schism and reunion, of conflict and
reconciliation. Cowan examined the intra-denomina-
tional aspects of the Presbyterian Church (PCUSA), the
United Methodist Church (UMC), and The Episcopal
Church (TEC), which he said were all "standing on the
edge of a precipice, staring chaos in the face."

According to some orthodox Episcopalians, the
theological "tipping point" for TEC occurred in 1965,
when TEC Bishop James Pike of California openly
denied the virgin birth and the resurrection of Jesus;
and the TEC House of Bishops refused to discipline him. Twenty-five years later, at TEC's General

Convention in Phoenix, Arizona, a majority of the TEC bishops passed "Resolution A104" that tacitly approved of the ordination of homosexual priests. The passage of this resolution ultimately paved the way for the consecration of Gene Robinson as TEC's first non-celibate homosexual bishop in 2003. The Presbyterian Church USA passed a similar resolution in May 2011.

The Anglican Communion's Response to the Robinson Consecration

Following Gene Robinson's consecration as the Bishop of New Hampshire in October 2003, 22 of the 38 provinces of the wider Anglican Communion joined together to condemn the "rebellious and erroneous actions of TEC," which they deemed "contrary to the teaching of the Anglican Communion and a departure from 5,000 years of Judeo-Christian teaching and practice." Even though several ERMs had evolved within The Episcopal Church during the latter half of the 20th century, the efforts of these ERMs had been unable to reverse the trend within TEC toward theological inclusiveness and liberalism.

Cowan explained this ineffectiveness in this way: "For a variety of reasons, [these ERMs] had not been successful in attracting the majority of their constituent denominations to their cause. These denominations were less in danger of splitting than they were of simply withering away . . . [because] a schism would have required far more energy than many of the mainline churches had to invest at that time". However, one ERM with The Episcopal Church, the North American Missionary Society (NAMS) had ample "energy" for schism if that is what it took to get TEC's attention.

The North American Missionary Society (NAMS)

In 1994, the Rev. Jon Shuler, a TEC priest in Knoxville, Tennessee and the General Secretary of the North American Missionary Society (NAMS) asked Chuck Murphy, the rector of All Saints Church in Pawleys Island, if he and his parish would become a partner in NAMS. Unlike most North American missionary movements, NAMS was a missionary movement *to* North America not *from* North America. Two years later, Jon Shuler moved the headquarters of NAMS onto the campus of All Saints Church and along with him came a young priest named Thaddeus Barnum.

Thaddeus Barnum, a graduate of Yale Divinity School, had served under Terry Fullam at St. Paul's, Darien before he and his wife, Erilynne, left Connecticut to plant a new church outside of Pittsburgh, Pennsylvania. In his book, *Never Silent*, Barnum tells the story of how he met John Rucyahana, an African priest who was studying at Trinity School for Ministry in Pittsburgh. Soon thereafter, Thad and Erilynne became affiliated with NAMS, and they moved to Pawleys Island where Thad joined the staff of All Saints Church.

Jon Shuler, Thad Barnum, and John Rucyahana are the unsung heroes of the Breakaway Anglican Church Movement. But for NAMS and Thad Barnum's relationship with John Rucyahana, the Singapore Consecrations may not have occurred.

The Consecration of Gene Robinson Produced Another ERM Within TEC: the ACN

Three months after Gene Robinson's consecration, in January 2004, a new ERM was established within TEC. Bob Duncan, the Bishop of Pittsburgh, and eleven other TEC bishops gathered in Plano, Texas and formed the Anglican Communion Network (the "ACN").

In 2004, the ACN became the *inside strategy*, while The Anglican Mission remained the *outside strategy* for dealing with an increasingly apostate Episcopal Church.

New Religious Movements (NRMs)

New religious movements, or NRMs (like The Anglican Mission), did not originate in the 21st century. Sociologists of religion William Sims Bainbridge, Rodney Stark, and Larry Iannaccone have all written extensively about "new religious movements" and what they call *church-sect theory* or the *church-sect cycle*. "Church-sect theory" maintains that, over time, religious organizations gradually reduce their tension with the surrounding social and cultural environment; and as a result, a counter-cultural process of religious revival and innovation begins that often produces one or more new religious movements.

For example, the "Methodist Miracle" was a response to the cultural accommodation of the Church of England in the 18th and 19th centuries, and the "Holiness Movement" was a response to the cultural accommodation of the Methodist Church in the United States during the twentieth century. Thus, according to Bainbridge:

> The model of the circulation of sects [NRMs] and denominations says that secularization is self-limiting, calling forth revivals that restore the existing religious tradition. Yet, we know that, throughout history, entirely new religious [movements] have arisen.

The Anglican Mission in the Americas (the Anglican Mission) is an example of an entirely new religious movement, one that evolved in response to the cultural accommodation of The Episcopal Church in the United States. Before examining the political and juridical contexts in which this new religious movement evolved, the next two chapters will look at the place where the movement began and the man behind the movement.

4

Pawleys Island and All Saints Church: The Birthplace of the Movement

The roots of the The Anglican Mission were embedded deeply in the soil of the coastal hamlet known as Pawleys Island, South Carolina and in a colonial Anglican church known as All Saints Church, Waccamaw, or simply, All Saints Church. According to the sign that greets you as you enter Pawleys Island, it is the "oldest seaside resort in America." Pawleys Island is also known for its "arrogantly shabby" beach cottages and for the Pawleys Island Rope Hammocks that were manufactured in the area for many years and exported all over the world. The history of Pawleys Island and of All Saints Church is robust, and it began during the 17th century when the "Province of Carolina" was established.

The Province of Carolina

Early French and Spanish explorers described the south Atlantic region of the *New World* as having a *sinister beauty* with its expanse of marshes and moss-draped live oak trees. Other explorers described the area as a *semi-tropical paradise, an Eden.*

After what some historians have described as a century of exploratory and colonial neglect on the part of England, King Charles I issued the first charter for the Province of Carolina in 1629. Additional charters were issued in 1663 and 1665 because it took the king three attempts to find settlers that were brave enough and hearty enough to survive in the *New World.*

The 1663 and 1665 provincial charters named eight true and absolute Lords and Proprietors and granted them virtually unlimited powers to settle the territory located south of Virginia and north of what is today Daytona Beach, Florida. The westward boundary of the Province of Carolina was the *South Seas* (the Pacific Ocean). The Province of Carolina contained 850,000 square miles of territory that today comprises 15 states and northern Mexico.

In 1682, the Lords and Proprietors divided the Province of Carolina into four counties: Berkeley County in the center that included Charles Town (Charleston), Colleton and Granville Counties to the south, and Craven County to the north that included Georgetown District and the area that would become Pawleys Island.

SOUTH CAROLINA
COUNTIES
1682-1785
CRAVEN 1682-1785
BERKELEY 1682-1785
COLLETON 1682-1785
GRANVILLE 1710-1785

Source: *South Carolina Abstracts,* Vol, III

The Lords and Proprietors promoted the settlement of Carolina by publishing fifteen promotional tracts that were distributed at the Carolina Coffee House on Birchin Lane in London. One-third of the tracts were translated into French in order to attract French Huguenots, and 27 of the first 36 land grants in Craven County were made to French Huguenots. By 1760, approximately 3,500 Welsh settlers had settled also in the Province of Carolina. One of those Welsh settlers was Percivell Pawley, a mariner.

The 1665 provincial charter authorized the Lords and Proprietors of the province *to build and found churches, chapels, and oratories in convenient and fit places.* The *Chapel at Waccamaw* was built on land owned by Percivell Pawley in what is today Pawleys Island. According to notes from the journal of the Rev. John Fordyce, the second rector of the *Parish of Prince George* (Georgetown): "The *Chapel of Waccamaw* had a large congregation and about 15 communicants during Lent 1737-1738" and "20 Communicants, Religious and Devout People in July 1741."

Percival Pawley and the Pawley Land Trust

In 1711, Percivell Pawley, the mariner, received 16 land grants in Craven County that totaled 2,800 acres. One of these grants was for 100 acres of land "bounding to the East on the Sea Marsh, to the South by land not laid out, and to the West on Waccamaw Creek." In his Last Will and Testament, Percivell Pawley devised 1,000 acres of his land in Craven County, including this 100 acre tract, to his son, Percival, a gunsmith. According to Percivell's Will, the 1,000 acres that he left his son also included "one great isle," presumably the area that is known today as Pawleys Island.

In 1745, Percival Pawley and his wife, Anna, conveyed 50 of the 1,000 acres to George Pawley (Percival's brother) and William Poole (a neighbor) *to be held forever in trust for the inhabitants of the Waccamaw Neck to be used as a church or chapel of the Church of England.* Pawleys Island lies within an area of land north of Winyah Bay and south of the North Carolina state line that is known as the *Waccamaw Neck* because of the contours made in the land by the Waccamaw River that runs through it.

Today, most church property is owned by non-profit *corporations*, but in the 17th and 18th centuries, church land was held in *land trusts*. The 50 acres that Percival and Anna Pawley conveyed to the Pawley Land Trust in 1745 (which was later determined by survey to be 60 acres) comprise the present day campus of All Saints Church.

Slavery and the Parish Churches

To the early *explorers*, the Carolina coast had appeared to be a paradise. To the early *settlers*, however, the vast forests and marshlands proved much too difficult to cultivate without the assistance of slave labor. By 1712, six hundred slaves per year were being imported into Carolina, and the number of slaves continued to increase faster than the number of *free whites.* According to the 1790 Census, the Georgetown District had twenty-two thousand residents of which thirteen thousand were slaves.

Therefore, the institution of slavery was an integral part of the growth and development of South Carolina; but, another institution, the church, ultimately became the glue that held the Province of Carolina together—culturally, politically, and spiritually. South Carolina historian George Rogers made the following observations about the culture, or lack thereof in Carolina:

> The bustle of frontier community provided little time for reflection and without reflection, there can be no culture. The people were engaged in getting and acquiring, not in thinking. . . . The chief civilizing agent in the early years was the church . . . . The cultural center, though at best a meager one, was the parish church.

The Church of England Fared Better in the Province of Carolina Than It Did In The Other Southern Colonies

The Church of England fared much better in the Province of Carolina than it did in the other southern colonies. The first Anglican church in South Carolina, St Philips, was established in Charles Town in 1681, and by 1768, twenty-two *parishes* of the Church of England had been established in South Carolina, including the *Parish of All Saints*.

During the 17th and 18th centuries, the *parish*, and its *parish church*, were the foundation of local government. Church wardens supervised the building of roads and the feeding of the poor, in addition to church matters. According to historian David Holmes:

> The Church of England especially attracted the plantation gentry, the professional class, urban merchants, and skilled craftsmen . . . . The vestry system was the foundation of local government; the wardens even supervised the elections to the legislature. Unlike the bustling seaport of Charles Town, Craven County had very few urban merchants, but the county had ample plantation gentry.

The Plantation Gentry and The Slave Chapels

Exports of indigo, and later of rice, resulted in Craven County becoming the wealthiest county in the United States during the late 1700s and early 1800s. Georgetown district, which included Pawleys Island, was the leading rice producing area in the United States, and 98 percent of the county's rice came from the plantations of 91 planters. The plantations of Joshua John Ward and Plowden C. J. Weston, who were both parishioners of the *Parish of All Saints*, each produced over one million pounds of rice per year.

In 1804, Plowden C. J. Weston's father, Francis Marion Weston, brought Alexander Glennie from Surrey, England to his plantation to serve as a tutor for his young son. Glennie soon became a lay reader at *All Saints Church*, and he was ordained a deacon in

43

1832 and a priest in 1833. According to the Rev. Henry D. Bull:

> The circumstances were ideal: a young energetic, consecrated priest, and with him working hand in hand, a devout layman of great ability and tremendous wealth, both devoted to the same ideal—the upbuilding of the church and the conversion of souls, black and white.

The devout layman that Bull was referring to was Plowden C. J. Weston, Glennie's former pupil who now owned several rice plantations in the *Parish of All Saints* and a great number of slaves. Weston thought of his slaves as "God's children to be brought to Jesus Christ, to be trained and instructed in the Christian way of life."

Under Glennie's supervision, Weston and several other planters on the Waccamaw Neck built thirteen "slave chapels" on their plantations of which St. Mary's Chapel (sometimes referred to as "Weston Chapel") on Hagley Plantation was the grandest. Bishop Philander Chase, a missionary bishop from the Midwest, made this entry in his journal after a visit to the Waccamaw Neck:

> The black children of a South Carolina planter know more of Christianity than thousands of white children in Illinois . . . . and the All Saints congregation is one of the largest, wealthiest and most permanent on the eastern seaboard, attached to their faithful rector, Dr. Glennie, and cooperating I believe in his labors of love for the negroes' souls.

The slaves attended the "slave chapels" constructed by the planters, but they also continued some of their religious customs from their native Africa. Another historian made this observation:

> Not far from Weston Chapel, on the Waccamaw River . . . is a "pray house" in which a so-called "class leader" conducts a service which it is well nigh impossible to describe . . . . There is shouting and clapping of hands and the most grotesque of physical conditions, often ending in some of the participants falling in a faint or trance, in which state they are carried to their homes.

The worldwide Pentecostal movement began in 1906 on Azuza Street in Los Angeles, California when William Joseph Seymour, an African American, was invited to become pastor of a holiness church there. However, the roots of the Pentecostal movement had been planted a century earlier in the soil of the southern plantations. Seymour's father was a slave on a rice plantation in Louisiana.

According to church historian Sydney Ahlstrom, the Church of England became a dominant tradition in South Carolina "not by force of popular vitality, but rather, because of governmental support and the social prominence of its membership." The *Parish of All Saints* also became a dominant tradition in the Low Country of South Carolina, as did many of its members.

The Parish of All Saints and the Episcopal Church of All Saints Parish

The *Parish of All Saints* was established in 1767 when the colonial *Assembly* passed the Parish Act of 1767. However, the *Board of Trade* in London disallowed the Act because the statute also provided for the addition of two representatives to the *Assembly*. After the *Revolutionary War*, the *Assembly* re-established the *Parish of All Saints* in 1778.

In 1819, the Rev. Henry Gibbes was chosen as the Rector of the *Parish of All Saints*, and he made this entry into his journal:

> Referring to the churches of All Saints' Parish, services are held on alternate Sundays . . . . the attendance is small, the number rarely exceeding 20 persons. There are no musical instruments and very few singers.

Gibbes' journal also revealed that the task of driving a carriage ten or twelve miles through heavy sand or traveling by boat three quarters of a mile up Chapel Creek to the parish church made it difficult to gather a congregation.

After the Revolution, several of the colonial parishes petitioned the *Assembly* for their own church *corporations* to be established. In 1820, the Vestry and Wardens of the *Parish of All Saints* asked the Assembly to issue a corporate charter in the name of the *Episcopal Church of All Saints Parish.* The Assembly issued the charter; however, the charter expired in 1839 and again in 1852. In 1852, the Assembly *revived* the charter of the *Episcopal Church of All Saints Parish* in perpetuity.

The Civil War and Total Destruction, Almost

The prosperity of the 18th and early 19th centuries dissipated rapidly following the Civil War (1861-1865). According to Bull, "Everything like order was broken up" at *All Saints Church* by the war. Bull added that Rev. Glennie "hung on for a year or so trying to restore some semblance of order and to gather his scattered flock . . . . but the old life of the kindly, wealthy planters, the busy rice culture, and the vast number of well-fed slaves was gone beyond recovery. The planters were reduced to poverty and *All Saints Church* was closed and deserted." A report of the Bishop of South Carolina stated: "The prostration of the once flourishing churches on Waccamaw is complete."

To outsiders, the destruction may have appeared complete, and countless historians have repeated these claims. However a careful review of the All Saints Church *Parish Register and Vestry Minute Book* revealed otherwise. Vestry meetings were held regularly from 1844 until 1893 (except for 1863,1864, and 1865) and wardens continued to be elected during these difficult times. Although the parish church was without a full-time rector on a number of occasions, the longest period between baptisms was twenty-five months.

During the last half of the 19th century, *All Saints Church* and its parishioners suffered greatly. Many of the once palatial rice plantation homes had been abandoned during the Civil War, and many of the remaining ones were destroyed by two devastating hurricanes that hit the coast of South Carolina in August and October of 1893. These hurricanes also devastated the finances of *All Saints Church.*

A New Corporate Charter and a Quit-Claim Deed

In 1902, the Vestry of All Saints Church attempted to sell a seventy-five foot strip of land on Pawleys Island to one H.H. Gardiner for $200. (A similar strip of land on Pawleys Island today would sell for well over $1 million dollars.) The conveyance to Mr. Gardiner could not be consummated because the corporate charter and the deed to the property had been destroyed during the hurricanes that devastated Pawleys Island in 1893.

All Saints Church needed to consummate the land transaction with Mr. Gardiner, so the Wardens asked the General Assembly to issue a new corporate charter. On June 21, 1902, a new corporate charter was issued to *All Saints Parish, Waccamaw*, and on May 30, 1903, representatives of the Episcopal Diocese of South Carolina executed a "quit-claim deed" to the new corporation for all of the church property owned then or formerly by the *Parish of All Saints* and *The Episcopal Church of All Saints*. The deed relinquished any rights that The Episcopal Church or the Diocese may have had to the property, and this quit-claim deed was cited by the Supreme Court of South Carolina in 2009 as one of the factors that it considered in its ruling that All Saints Church owned its 60 acre campus, and The Episcopal Church had no interest in its church property.

All Saints Church Looked Forward to Another Century of Service

In his definitive history of *All Saints Church,* The Rev. Henry D. Bull offered this concluding comment:

> All Saints, Church, Waccamaw, has lived out its long life in a small corner of this great country of ours, but it has been a life of great worth. For more than six generations the people of Waccamaw have gathered here and worshiped God and sung His praise. There have been many vicissitudes. Four great wars have come and gone. There have been periods of wealth and prosperity and of meager, desolating poverty, of wind and storm and fire and flood. It has been an honorable life blessed with the devoted service of brave godly men and women in every

decade. Today, All Saints Church, Waccamaw, set in the midst of the oaks and moss and azaleas of its ancient domain seems quietly and steadfastly to look forward to other centuries of service to the glory of God.

All Saints Church's Most Recent Century of Service

All Saints Church recovered from the devastation of the Civil War and the back-to-back hurricanes of 1893, but the congregation remained very small. A. H. "Doc" Lachicotte, Jr., the patriarch of the congregation, testified during the *All Saints Church* property litigation that he became the "ninth male" in the congregation when he returned to Pawleys Island after graduating from college in 1950. Gurdon Tarbox, the curator of nearby Brookgreen Gardens and a long-time member of *All Saints Church*, stated that "attendance" during the 1960s and 1970s rarely exceeded sixteen adults, even though the congregation supposedly had 178 "members."

However, things began to change radically in 1982, when the Vestry of *All Saints Church* called Charles Hurt Murphy, III, affectionately know as "Chuck", to become its twentieth rector and senior pastor. During *The Murphy* Years at All Saints Church (1982–2004), Chuck Murphy and his rag-tag army of believers transformed the tiny congregation of *All Saints Church* into one of the largest Episcopal churches in the United States for which he and the congregation gained national and international recognition. By 2003, average Sunday attendance at *All Saints Church* exceeded 800, and it became one of only three Episcopal congregations in the country that had grown ten-fold in ten years.

The news of the remarkable growth and transformation that had occurred at *All Saints Church* spread widely, and soon Episcopalians and Anglicans from all over the country and the world started coming to visit this unique church. One of the first questions that these visitors asked was: "Who is this Chuck Murphy? Where did he come from?" The next chapter attempts to answer those questions.

5

CHUCK MURPHY:
THE MAN BEHIND
THE MOVEMENT

Anglicans had been worshiping on the campus of *All Saints Church* for over two hundred and fifty years when the Vestry called Chuck Murphy to become its twentieth rector.

In 1982, when Chuck Murphy arrived in Pawleys Island, the population was 3,446, and the community had one traffic light that flashed caution after dark. Chuck Murphy referred to Pawleys Island as "Hooterville" and to his hand full of parishioners as his "rag-tag army." Twenty-three years later, when Chuck Murphy stepped down as Rector, the population had increased to 10,309.

In 1982, when Chuck Murphy became the twentieth rector of *All Saints Church*, average Sunday attendance was approximately 75, which is typical for Episcopal congregations. Twenty-two years later, average Sunday attendance at *All Saints Church* had increased to over 800 making *All Saints Church* one of the largest Episcopal congregations in the country.

Chuck Murphy and his rag-tag army had made a difference in the lives of many who resided in Hooterville. Who was this Chuck Murphy, and where did he come from?

Chuck Murphy—The Man

Chuck Murphy was born and educated in Alabama. His father was a professional musician prior to becoming an Episcopal priest. After completing five years of undergraduate studies (and partying, according to his wife, Margaret) at the University of Alabama, Murphy spent a year in banking, during which he contemplated a career in law or ministry.

According to Murphy: "I thought that I had the gifts and the skill-set to be successful as a lawyer or as a minister. I felt that I could entice people into the dance. I had watched my father do it for years, and I liked the results." So Murphy attended a diocesan discernment weekend that was sponsored by the Diocese of Alabama, and he scored the highest on the aptitude test for clergy of anyone in the history of the diocese. "This was very confirming for Margaret and me," Murphy said, "although Margaret was not really thrilled about becoming a preacher's wife."

The Rev. Tom Jones, an Episcopal priest in Alabama, introduced Chuck Murphy to the Rev. John Guest, an English priest who became, first the youth director and later, the Rector of St. Stephens Episcopal Church in Sewickley, Pennsylvania, a suburb of Pittsburgh. Guest also helped establish Trinity School of Ministry in Pittsburgh, Pennsylvania. Trinity Seminary has become one the last bastions of orthodoxy and evangelicalism within The Episcopal Church and annually sends theologically conservative graduates into Episcopal and

Anglican churches throughout the United States and more recently into Africa.

The Influence of James I. Packer and Pip "n" Jay

Tom Jones and John Guest had studied under Dr. J. I. Packer at Tyndale Hall, in Bristol, England, and they encouraged Murphy to do the same. So Chuck Murphy attended Tyndale Hall where Dr. Packer served as his personal tutor. "It was an awesome experience," Murphy said, "because I got to sit with Packer, one on one, every Friday. I had to be prepared because, unlike in my undergraduate classes, I knew that I would be called on to answer questions about the material."

While Chuck Murphy was studying in Bristol, Tyndale Hall merged with Dalton House and Clifton to become Trinity College. According to Murphy, Dr. Packer was a classical evangelical. Unlike John Stott and some of his Anglican contemporaries, Packer was much more receptive to the Pentecostal movement that was evolving within the Church of England at the time. Packer saw the hand of God at work in the Pentecostal movement.

In 1971, Packer sent Chuck Murphy into the inner city of Bristol to experience the worship at the historic parish church of St. Philip and St Jacob, also known as Pip 'n' Jay. Pip 'n' Jay had been a parish of the Church of England since at least 1174 when it was one of the fiefs of William, Earl of Gloucester. During the eighteenth century, Pip 'n' Jay had welcomed such noteworthy preachers as John and Charles Wesley and George Whitefield to its pulpit. However, following World War II, the size of the congregation declined rapidly.

The membership of the parish had dwindled to seventeen when the assistant curate, the Rev. Malcolm Widdecombe, began leading a small group of young people in enthusiastic worship on Sunday evenings. Widdecombe became one of the pioneers of the charismatic movement in England, and what Chuck Murphy observed at Pip 'n' Jay would become an integral part of his own worship style and ministry. According to Murphy:

> At Pip 'n' Jay, Malcolm Widdecombe was able to create a space and a place to encounter God, within the framework and trappings of the Anglican liturgy. The world was crying out for an encounter with God. It was longing for transcendence, and Malcolm opened a window to it in the classical Anglican liturgy. He was able to create an opportunity for his members to experience the transcendence of the living God.

Widdecombe and his wife Meryl continued to lead the worship at Pip 'n' Jay for over forty years until Malcolm's death in 2010. Unlike many Church of England services, the services at Pip 'n' Jay were always well attended by enthusiastic members from many nationalities and socioeconomic levels. When asked about his efforts to create a space within the Anglican liturgy for people to experience God, Widdecombe responded:

> The liturgy is not our master. It is our servant. We should enjoy it. After the benediction, we don't say amen; we shout and clap! There was a time when I couldn't stand the Pentecostals, then I became one.

Following a well-attended Sunday evening worship service at Pip 'n' Jay, the Widdecombes reminisced about their encounter with Chuck and Margaret Murphy. They recalled many late-night chats while the Murphys lived with them in the nine-bedroom vicarage until housing became available at Trinity College. "I knew that Chuck would do well," Malcolm said. "I asked him to give his testimony one night, and he did a splendid job. He preached his first sermon here too." Meryl said that she understood that Chuck Murphy had become somewhat of a maverick within TEC and the Anglican Communion. She added enthusiastically: "Chuck Murphy is a rebel because he was taught by a rebel."

J. I. Packer, Chuck Murphy's advisor at Trinity College, is presently the Board of Governors' Professor of Theology at Regent College, Vancouver, Canada. Packer preached at *All Saints Church* on several occasions, and he always referred to Chuck Murphy as "one of my boys." However, according to Dr. Packer, Chuck Murphy was an average student with no particular agenda while he was at Trinity College. Therefore, he was pleasantly surprised to learn of Murphy's involvement, nationally and internationally, first in the affairs of TEC, and later in the Anglican Mission and the wider Anglican Communion.

After spending a year at Trinity College under Packer's tutelage, Murphy had exhausted his savings. Thus, he and his wife, Margaret, returned to the United States, so that he could complete his theological education at Sewanee Seminary in Tennessee. The foundation in classical Anglican theology that Chuck Murphy had received at Trinity College did not mesh well with the revisionist theology that was then being propagated at Sewanee.

Chuck Murphy defined classical Anglican theology as *the faith once delivered to the Saints*, and he recalled his time at Sewanee with some angst. He noted: "I was deemed unteachable by the faculty and staff at Sewanee, but by God's grace, I graduated."

Murphy Taught the Theology of Stewardship to TEC Parishes Around the U.S.

While Chuck Murphy was still in seminary at Sewanee, the Diocese of Alabama invited some of the best and the brightest professional fund raisers in the country to a symposium on stewardship for the clergy. According to Chuck:

> I was impressed with the fund raising tools and techniques that were presented by these experts, but I felt that the theology piece was missing. The professionals presented the concepts, but there was no teaching based on Scripture. I did not want to sell the concept to members. I wanted to explain it to them. I wanted them to understand the Biblical basis for giving. So, I devised my own apologetics, using Ezekiel 36 and Jeremiah 31, and they began to catch on.

Murphy's apologetics were so compelling that he began to receive invitations to teach stewardship at Episcopal churches around the country. He accepted many of these invitations, and the observations that he made while visiting the various churches proved invaluable to him in his later ministry. "I got to see the best parishes with the brightest leaders because they could afford me, and I got to see some of the worst ones because they desperately needed me. I was able to observe what these churches did well, and I also saw what they did pitifully."

Chuck Murphy continued to teach stewardship to members of Episcopal congregations throughout the United States for fifteen years after he became Rector of *All Saints Church*. Later, priests and vestries from sixty-nine different TEC congregations from around the country visited All Saints Church to see for themselves how this tiny colonial congregation had been transformed into one of the largest TEC churches in the country. When the crisis of faith and leadership evolved in TEC during the late 1990s, Chuck Murphy invited many of these same priests and leaders to return to All Saints Church for a time of prayer and discernment. Today, many of these same priests and congregations form the core of The Anglican Mission.

The Crisis of Faith and Leadership Within The Episcopal Church and The First Promise Roundtable

In *The Gathering Storm*, sociologist Jeffrey Hadden described a storm that had hit the American mainline churches with a vengeance in the 1960s. According to Hadden, the churches in the United States (and in the United Kingdom) were presented with a threefold crisis: a crisis of meaning and purpose, a crisis of belief, and a crisis of authority.

In 1997, as the crisis of faith and leadership was evolving within The Episcopal Church, Chuck Murphy invited 30 theologically conservative Episcopal bishops, priests, and lay leaders from around the country to a meeting at *All Saints Church* in order to discuss the crisis and to discern what if anything could be done to combat it. Murphy had not read *The Gathering Storm*, but since his ordination as an Episcopal priest, he had witnessed first-hand the growing crisis of faith and leadership that was developing within The Episcopal Church precisely as Hadden had predicted that it would almost forty years earlier.

This group of theologically conservative Episcopalian leaders that met at *All Saints Church* in 1997 met again in 1998 and formed the *First Promise Roundtable* which led to the consecration in Singapore of Chuck Murphy and John Rodgers as "Missionary Bishops" *to* the United States in January 2000. Later that year, The Anglican Mission was established as a "missionary outreach" of the Anglican Church of Rwanda.

The Anglican Mission—A Movement with a Mission

The Anglican Mission began as and continues to be a *movement with a mission.* According to Chuck Murphy, the mission of the Anglican Mission was two-fold: (1) to reach the approximately 130 million unchurched Americans with the Gospel of Jesus Christ, and (2) to offer an alternative to other orthodox Episcopal priests and congregations who decided that they could no longer remain within The Episcopal Church. During its first ten years, the Anglican Mission planted 252 theologically conservative Anglican congregations throughout the United States and Canada, an average of one new congregation every three weeks.

The remaining chapters of this book will examine the political and juridical contexts in which these break-away Anglican churches and The Anglican Mission emerged.

6

The Emergence of the Breakaway Anglican Churches

I n *The Gathering Storm,* Jeffrey Hadden observed that the decentralized nature of Protestantism in the United States prevented many church leaders and the vast majority of the churchgoing public from grasping the depth or the complexity of the growing crisis in faith and leadership within their churches. Despite massive declines in membership for over thirty years, the majority of the members of TEC had not recognized the severity of the crisis of faith and leadership that existed within their church. However, this circumstance began to change within TEC in January 2000 when two TEC priests were consecrated in Singapore as "missionary bishops" *to the United States*.

For over two hundred years, churches in the United States had sent Christian missionaries to Africa, Asia, and Latin America. However, on January 29, 2000, the Most Rev. Moses Tay, Archbishop of Southeast Asia, and the Most Rev. Emmanuel Kolini, Archbishop of Rwanda, Africa, reversed that trend. These two archbishops declared the West, specifically the United States and Canada, to be the new "mission field." These archbishops, along with the Rt. Rev. David Pytches of England, the Rt. Rev. John Rucyahana of Rwanda, The Rt. Rev. FitzSimmons Allison and the Rt. Rev. Alex Dickson of the United States, consecrated Charles H. Murphy, III and John H. Rodgers, Jr. as "missionary bishops" to the United States.

The Birth of The Anglican Mission and The Network

Eight months later, in August 2000, the archbishops encouraged Bishops Murphy and Rodgers to establish the Anglican Mission in America (The Anglican Mission) as a missionary outreach of the Anglican Church of Rwanda to the over 130 million unchurched Americans and to orthodox Episcopalians who decided that they could no longer remain in TEC. Thus, The Anglican Mission soon became a vehicle for providing "alternative episcopal oversight" to these orthodox Episcopalians in the United States who had recognized the crisis of faith and leadership that existed within their church and wished to move their "canonical residence" to another church within the Anglican Communion.

In 2004, another movement, The Network of Anglican Communion Dioceses and Parishes (the "Network"), was established by the Rt. Rev. Robert Duncan, the TEC Bishop of Pittsburgh. The Network was made up of orthodox priests and parishes that had chosen to remain within TEC in hopes that the Primates of the Anglican Communion would create a new orthodox Anglican province within North America. Therefore, The Anglican Mission represented the "outside strategy" for reaching out to these orthodox

Episcopalians, while the Network represented the "inside strategy."

The epiphany for most American Episcopalians concerning the state of their church came in 2003 when TEC consecrated Gene Robinson, a non-celibate homosexual, as the Bishop of New Hampshire. Many orthodox Episcopalians were stunned by Robinson's consecration; however, the orthodox bishops within TEC were not surprised.

The 1991 TEC General Convention was the "Tipping Point"

According to the Rt. Rev. Alex Dickson, retired bishop of West Tennessee, the theological "tipping point" from orthodoxy toward revisionism within TEC occurred at the TEC General Convention in Phoenix in 1991. According to Bishop Dickson, the TEC House of Bishops met in September 1990 and voted 78 to 74 to prohibit the ordination and consecration of practicing homosexuals. However, ten months later at the General Convention, the House of Bishops reversed its earlier decision by a vote of 93 to 85.

The orthodox bishops asked for a roll call, and an analysis of the votes revealed that 14 of the 15 bishops that had been consecrated since September 1990 had voted in favor of consecrating practicing homosexuals. Therefore, according to Bishop Dickson, the 1991 TEC General Convention could be considered the "tipping-point"—the precise point at which the liberal revisionist bishops gained control of the House of Bishops of TEC.

The Hope and the Future Conference: Pittsburgh, November 2005

In November 2005, two years after the Robinson Consecration, over 2,400 Episcopalians from 77 dioceses throughout the United States attended the "Hope and a Future Conference" in Pittsburgh, Pennsylvania. The conference was sponsored by The Network and was hosted by the Rt. Rev. Robert Duncan, the TEC Bishop of Pittsburgh. The conference was also attended by 9 Anglican archbishops, 47 diocesan bishops, and 325 Episcopal priests. Bob Duncan looked regal in his flowing robes as he followed the procession of archbishops, bishops, and priests into the main hall for the opening worship service. Five years later, Duncan was installed as the Archbishop of the Anglican Church of North America.

The orthodox Episcopal leaders who attended the Hope and a Future Conference were told by Bishop Duncan that a crisis of faith and leadership existed in their church, and that the purpose of the conference was to discuss the "re-alignment of the leadership" of TEC.

The conference participants heard the Rt. Rev. Keith Ackerman, Bishop of Quincy and President of Forward in Faith North America (FiFNA), an association of theologically conservative Anglo-Catholic churches in the United States, assert that TEC had started down the road to apostasy in 1965 when the Rt. Rev. James Pike, Bishop of California, announced that he no longer believed in the Trinity, and the TEC House of Bishops had refused to exercise their canonical right to discipline him.

Next, Anglican Archbishops Yong of Southeast Asia, Orombi of Uganda, and Akinola of Nigeria described the explosive growth of orthodox Anglicanism in their countries. Archbishop Akinola declared:

> This is your moment to make up our mind. Many of you have one leg in The Episcopal Church and one leg in the Network. If you really want the Global South to partner with you, you must let us know exactly where you stand. Are you an Episcopalian, or are you [in the] Network?

The crowd roared with approval, and gave Archbishop Akinola a standing ovation.

In the weeks following the Hope and a Future Conference, TEC parishes in California, Connecticut, and Florida announced that they could no longer remain within The Episcopal Church. Following the TEC General Convention in June 2006, where Katherine Jefferts Schori was elected as the first female Presiding Bishop and the first female Primate within the Anglican Communion, four entire dioceses announced that they were seeking "alternative primatial oversight" (APO).

Soon thereafter, the largest TEC parish, Christ Church, Plano in Dallas, Texas, and eleven parishes in Virginia that represented 25 percent of the Episcopalians in the Diocese of Virginia, also sought "alternative Episcopal oversight" (AEO). The table below contains the number of "Breakaway Anglican Churches" and the number of "Network" congregations in the United States as of January 2007.

"Breakaway Anglican Churches" and "Network"
Churches in the United States as of January 2007

Number	Affiliation
120	Alternative Episcopal Oversight-Anglican Mission
40	Alternative Episcopal Oversight-Other
202	Anglican Communion Network Parishes
362	Total Anglican Mission and Network Parishes

Source: www.amia.org and www.acn-us.org. The 40 "other" parishes that have obtained 'alternative episcopal oversight' are 'Anglican Communion Partners' of the Network.

The seventh annual "Anglican Mission Winter Conference" was held in January 2007. Archbishops from eight provinces attended the conference. Chairman Chuck Murphy announced that the Anglican Mission had changed its name from the "Anglican Mission in America" to the "Anglican Mission in the Americas" to denote its expansion into Canada. Following the conference, Christ Church, Plano, the largest TEC congregation in the United States, announced that it was affiliating with the Anglican Mission. Therefore, by January 2007, a realignment of the leadership of TEC was clearly in progress. The next two chapters will examine the political and juridical contexts within which this realignment and the "Breakaway Anglican Churches" emerged.

7

The Anglican Communion: The Political Contexts in which the Breakaway Anglican Churches Emerged

The Anglican Communion traces its roots to A.D. 597 when St. Augustine became the first Archbishop of Canterbury. The present Archbishop of Canterbury, the Most Rev. Rowan Williams, was enthroned as the 104th Archbishop of Canterbury on February 27, 2003. In 2011, the Anglican Communion had 38 provinces that were located around the world. Like TEC, most of the provinces in the Anglican Communion were either successors to, or vestiges of, colonial parishes of the Church of England.

The Archbishop of Canterbury serves as the titular head of the Anglican Communion, and he is considered the "first among equals" by his peers. Although the Archbishop of Canterbury has no governing authority, he is considered one of the four "Instruments of Unity" of the Anglican Communion in that he: (1) convenes the decennial Lambeth Conferences, (2) chairs the meetings of Primates, and (3) serves as President of the Anglican Consultative Council.

The bishops of the Anglican churches that are "in communion" with the See of Canterbury typically are invited by the Archbishop of Canterbury to attend the decennial "Lambeth Conferences." The first Lambeth Conference was held in 1867. The Lambeth Conference of 1888 adopted the "Lambeth Quadrilateral," a statement that set forth "the principles of unity exemplified by the undivided Catholic Church" and a set of principles that represented "the substantial deposit of the Christian Faith and Order committed by Christ and the Apostles to the Church." The Clergy of the Breakaway Anglican Churches maintained that TEC had departed from these principles—from the "faith once delivered to the Saints."'

<u>The 1998 Lambeth Conference was the Theological Tipping Point for the Anglican Communion</u>

Just as the 1991 TEC General Convention became a theological "tipping point" for TEC, the 1998 Lambeth Conference became a theological (and political) "tipping point" for the Anglican Communion. At the 1998 Lambeth Conference, the "third worlders" (the delegates from Africa, Asia and Latin America) made their voices heard. Historically, the adage used to describe Lambeth Conferences had been: "The Americans pay, the Africans pray, and the British draft the resolutions." However, the Africans (and other bishops from the Global South) intended to do more than just pray at the 1998 Lambeth Conference. In preparation for Lambeth 1998, the Primates from the southern hemisphere held two "Encounters in the South."

The Second Encounter in the South: Kuala Lumpur, February 1997

The second of these encounters was held in Kuala Lumpur, Malaysia in February 1997 and was attended by eighty bishops from thirty different nations. The delegates at Kuala Lumpur unanimously endorsed a "Statement on Human Sexuality" that became known as the "Kuala Lumpur Statement." The following are excerpts from the Kuala Lumpur Statement:

> With an awareness of our own vulnerability to sexual sin, we express our profound concern about recent developments relating to Church discipline and moral teaching in some provinces in the North – specifically the ordination of practicing homosexuals and the blessing of same-sex unions.
>
> The Holy Scriptures are clear in teaching that all sexual promiscuity is sin. We are convinced that this includes homosexual practices between men and women, as well as heterosexual relationships outside of marriage. This leads us to express concern about mutual accountability and interdependence within our Anglican Communion.

The "Kuala Lumpur Statement" put the Primates, and the other delegates to the 1998 Lambeth Conference, on notice that a break in communion was likely, if TEC and the Anglican Church of Canada were not held accountable for their recent actions. Absent "complete accountability and demonstrable repentance" on their part, communion and fellowship would be broken. Therefore, the stage was set as 736 bishops from 37 provinces of the Anglican Communion traveled to Lambeth for the 13th Lambeth Conference in July 1998.

The 1998 Lambeth Conference Adopted a Biblically-Based Statement on Human Sexuality

Of the 736 bishops who registered at the 1998 Lambeth Conference, 316 were from the United States, Canada, and Europe, and 319 were from Africa and Asia. According to the *Church Times,* the delegation from the Global South was fully in control during the debate on homosexuality. "By every reckoning," the *Church Times* observed, "'it was a pivotal moment in the life of the Anglican Communion." A consortium of bishops from Africa, Asia, and Latin America, who were joined by conservative bishops from the United States, succeeded in having the conference adopt a biblically-based statement on human sexuality. The vote was 526 to 70 with 45 abstentions.

The reactions by the delegates from the provinces in the northern hemisphere ranged from surprise to outrage. For example, TEC Bishop John Spong of Newark, New Jersey, declared that the African Bishops had "moved out of animism into a very superstitious kind of Christianity" that prevented them from fully comprehending the issues at hand. Fifty orthodox TEC Bishops had declared two months earlier that it was Spong, not the Africans, who had left the Anglican faith. Spong was not alone in ridiculing the Lambeth resolution on human sexuality.

In the weeks following the conference, other TEC bishops joined the debate. Spong's successor in Newark, Bishop Kroneberger, announced that he would proceed with the preparation of liturgy for same-sex blessings. Bishop Knudsen of Maine told her diocese that the action of the Lambeth Conference had no legislative effect. Bishop Jelinek of Minnesota said that no changes would be made in his diocese as a result of the Lambeth resolution. Bishop Borsch of Los

Angeles, who had already ordained thirty openly gay priests, said that he would continue to ordain "human beings" adding that he would not discriminate based on sexual orientation. By the fall of 1998, twenty TEC bishops and dioceses had formally repudiated the Lambeth Conference resolution on human sexuality.

The First Promise Roundtable

In September 1997 and in December 1998, Chuck Murphy, the Rector of All Saints Church, called together a broad coalition of orthodox TEC leaders whose stated goal was to "preserve the Anglican faith in the United States of America." The members of this coalition, the *First Promise Roundtable,* were united in their submission to the sovereign authority of Holy Scripture, the historic Creeds, the traditional Faith of the Prayer Book, the resolutions of the 1998 Lambeth Conference, and the Kuala Lumpur Statement.

Following their initial meeting on the campus of All Saints Church in Pawleys Island, South Carolina, the *First Promise Roundtable* issued the following statement:

> We are proud to be Anglicans in the mainstream of the Communion, but we find ourselves increasingly marginalized and theologically offended in TEC. Some in revisionist (unorthodox) dioceses are under attack from revisionist bishops and under threat of presentment and trial.

> We have read with thanksgiving the following petitions dated December 1998 made by the Association of Anglican Congregations on Mission:

PETITION TO THE PRIMATES' MEETING AND THE PRIMATES OF THE ANGLICAN COMMUNION FOR EMERGENCY INTERVENTION IN THE PROVINCE OF THE EPISCOPAL CHURCH OF THE UNITED STATES OF AMERICA.

PETITION TO ORTHODOX BISHOPS OF THE ANGLICAN COMMUNION FOR PROTECTION OF ORTHODOX ANGLICANS IN THE UNITED STATES UNTIL THE EPISCOPAL CHURCH OF THE UNITED STATES OF AMERICA IS REFORMED OR REPLACED AS A PROVINCE OF THE COMMUNION.

Each of us personally agrees with and supports these petitions and seeks the relief requested therein.

TEC's Presiding Bishop Griswold Invited the Primates to "Come, See, and Listen"

In January 1999, following the 1998 Lambeth Conference, an "Open Letter" was sent to TEC's Presiding Bishop Frank Griswold by a group of Primates from the Global South who expressed concern at what appeared to be a "significant expression of dissent" by a number of TEC bishops to the 1998 Lambeth Resolution on human sexuality. Griswold responded in March 1999 by inviting the Primates to "come, see, and listen."

Archbishop Maurice Sinclair of the Southern Cone (Latin America) and Archbishop Harry Goodhew of Sydney accepted Griswold's invitation, along with bishops from Tanzania, Kenya, and Rwanda. Following their visit, the five bishops issued a report of their findings to Griswold. They stated:

We find that the [TEC] House of Bishops finds dif-
ficulty in exercising discipline. . . . . We were made
aware of fears that the General Convention to be
held next year in Denver would see changes made in
areas of accepted moral teaching. People expressed
a concern that this would mark a point beyond which
they would be forced either to leave [TEC] or to seek
other forms of Episcopal oversight.

The Singapore Consecrations

Having read the visiting bishops' report to Griswold,
and knowing that they had to act prior to the Denver
General Convention, the Most Rev. Dr. Moses Tay,
Archbishop of the Province of South East Asia, and The
Most Rev. Emmanuel Kolini, Archbishop of the Province
of Rwanda, called for the consecration of Charles H.
Murphy, III and John H. Rodgers, Jr. in Singapore on
January 29, 2000 as "Missionary Bishops" to the United
States and Canada.

In a letter to the Archbishop of Canterbury dated
January 30, 2000, Archbishops Tay and Kolini stressed
that the Singapore consecrations were an "interim
action to provide pastoral assistance and nurture to
faithful individuals and [TEC] congregations." The
Archbishops added:

The present conditions in the ECUSA [TEC] have
produced an "intolerable situation" involving the
"misuse of provincial autonomy", ongoing "innovations exceeding the limits of our Anglican diver-
sity," and Christian standards that are now "being
notoriously breached". . . . We have simply acted
in response to a request by the American Anglican
Council (AAC) bishops for intervention.

The Rt. Rev. C. FitzSimmons Allison, retired Bishop of the Diocese of South Carolina, and the Rt. Rev. Alex D. Dickson, retired Bishop of West Tennessee, also participated in the Singapore Consecrations. Bishops Allison and Dickson said in a press release issued following the consecrations that they were led to participate because of the crisis of faith and leadership in TEC. According to these two retired TEC bishops:

The crisis is two-fold: Faith and Leadership.

Faith – TEC's explicit denials of the Apostolic Faith as expressed in Scripture, Creeds, Councils and Anglican formularies.

Leadership – the failure of the TEC House of Bishops to maintain the limits and boundaries of "the Faith which was once delivered to the Saints" that is essential to our authentic unity.

Because of this crisis, innumerable clergy and laity have already left The Episcopal Church.

Bishops Murphy and Rodgers also issued a statement saying that they hoped to "lead TEC back to its Biblical foundations."

The first shot that was fired in the United States Civil War was fired from Fort Sumter in Charleston, South Carolina. The first shot in the "theological war" between the revisionist bishops of TEC and the orthodox Archbishops of the Anglican Communion was fired from All Saints Church in Pawleys Island, South Carolina with the Singapore Consecrations.

The TEC 2000 General Convention in Denver

Six months later, the TEC 2000 General Convention began in Denver, and the liberal bishops pressed on with their agenda. By a vote of 119 to 19, the House of Bishops approved resolution D039 which "provided a safe and just structure . . . . for 'couples' in the Body of Christ and in this Church, who are living in marriage and in *other life-long committed relationships* [emphasis added]." The House of Bishops also approved the following resolution concerning rites for same-sex unions:

> Resolved, that desiring to support relationships of mutuality and fidelity other than marriage which mediate the Grace of God, [this convention] directs the Standing Commission on Liturgy and Music to prepare rites by means of which the Church may express that support.

However, the House of Deputies, the lay delegates, narrowly defeated the resolution dealing with rites for same-sex unions.

In a report to the All Saints Church congregation following the Denver Convention, Senior Warden and convention delegate A. H. "Doc" Lachicotte, Jr. said: "For the first time in my life, I have to say that I am ashamed to be an Episcopalian." Such a statement would have been a bold one coming from any Episcopalian; however, Lachicotte was the Senior Warden of All Saints Church and had served on its Vestry since the 1950s. Lachicotte was also the acknowledged patriarch of the parish.

The Denver Consecrations

If the Singapore Consecrations had been the "first shot across the liberal bark," the TEC liberal bishops had returned fire at the General Convention in Denver. Almost one year later, Archbishops Emmanuel Kolini of Rwanda and Datuk Yong Ping Chung (Archbishop Moses Tay's successor) of South East Asia raised the stakes by choosing Denver as the site to consecrate four additional American priests as Anglican Mission "missionary bishops": the Rev. Thaddeus Barnum of Pawleys Island, the Rev. Alexander Greene of Colorado, the Rev. Thomas Johnston of Arkansas, and the Rev. Doug Weiss of California.

A spokesman for the Archbishop of Canterbury stated that the consecrations had gone ahead despite Dr. Carey's "strong but businesslike" appeal to the Archbishops not to proceed. TEC Presiding Bishop Frank Griswold made the following comment:

> Consecrating bishops in the United States without informing me and certainly without my permission . . . is a profound violation of what it means to live in communion and could have drastic negative effects within our Anglican fellowship.

The American Anglican Council (the "AAC"), a group of orthodox bishops and laity who had chosen to remain in TEC, and who had been supportive of the Singapore Consecrations, criticized the Denver Consecrations as divisive. Others objected to the consecrations because two of the four bishops that were consecrated, Johnston and Barnum, had served as Chuck Murphy's associates at All Saints Church. These critics intimated that Murphy and The Anglican Mission had selected and approved the candidates, rather than the House of Bishops of Rwanda as required by canon law.

The Church of England Entered the Fray

The Church of England, not TEC, fired the next shot in the continuing battle over human sexuality within the Anglican Communion. The Bishop of Oxford, Richard Harries, appointed Dr. Jeffrey John, an openly gay priest, to serve as the Bishop of Reading, in the Diocese of Oxford. Following weeks of bitter argument within the Church of England about whether or not he should be allowed to hold the position, Canon John withdrew his acceptance of the appointment "because of the damage [my] consecration might cause to the unity of the church." His consecration had been scheduled for October 9, 2003.

The Consecration of V. Gene Robinson as TEC's First Openly Gay Bishop

Less than one month after Canon John withdrew his acceptance of the appointment as Bishop of Reading, TEC convened its 2003 General Convention in Minneapolis. On August 5, 2003, in Minneapolis, a majority of the TEC House of Bishops elected the Rev. Gene Robinson, a non-celibate gay priest, who openly lived with his "partner," to become the next Bishop of New Hampshire. Robinson had been narrowly defeated for the episcopacy in the Diocese of Newark and the Diocese of Rochester at earlier TEC General Conventions. Therefore, the revisionist bishops in the House of Bishops had finally been able to muster the necessary votes for Robinson's election as TEC's first openly gay bishop.

Immediately following Robinson's election, the orthodox bishops within TEC appealed to the

Archbishop of Canterbury for relief, and a special meeting of the Primates of the 38 provinces, was held at Lambeth Palace October 14-16, 2003. TEC's Presiding Bishop Frank Griswold attended this special meeting, and the Primates urged Griswold to delay Robinson's consecration. Griswold refused citing a lack of "canonical authority" to do so. Therefore, in a ceremony full of pomp and circumstance, the Rev. Gene Robinson was consecrated as TEC's first openly gay bishop on November 2, 2003.

The "Eames Commission" and the *"ius commune"* of the Anglican Communion

Those Primates who had attended the October meeting at Lambeth Palace had expressed their unanimous commitment to the ongoing life of the Anglican Communion, despite the fact that a state of impaired or broken communion was beginning to exist. The Primates also requested that the Archbishop of Canterbury establish a commission to study the issue of "human sexuality and communion among the provinces" and to report its findings within one year.

On October 28, 2003, the Archbishop of Canterbury appointed five Archbishops and twelve other Anglican leaders to serve on what became known as the "Eames Commission" because Archbishop Robin Eames, the Primate of All Ireland, was asked to serve as its chair. Archbishop Williams also appointed Professor Norman Doe, the Director of the Centre for Law and Religion at Cardiff University Law School, to serve on the Commission.

At a meeting of the Primates at Kanuga, North Carolina in March 2001, Professor Doe had presented a paper that suggested the possibility that a high degree of juridical similarity and unity existed among the churches of the Anglican Communion despite its lack of a constitution and canons. In response, the Primates had asked Professor Doe to further study the juridical systems of the 38 provinces in order to determine what similarities did indeed exist.

In March 2002, Professor Doe presented the preliminary findings of his study to the Anglican Communion Legal Advisors Consultation, a group of canon lawyers that the Archbishop of Canterbury had appointed to pursue this and other matters of canon law within the Communion. The Consultation tested Professor Doe's hypothesis and agreed that at least 44 "shared principles" could be induced from the juridical systems of the provinces within the Anglican Communion and further concluded that the existence of these "shared principles" constituted the "common law" or *ius commune* of the Anglican Communion.

Following a report of the Consultation's conclusions to the Primates' Meeting at Canterbury in April 2002, "the Primates recognized the unwritten law common to the Churches of the Communion and expressed that the shared principles of canon law may be understood to constitute a fifth 'instrument of unity'. ... Given that law may be understood to provide a basic framework to sustain the minimal conditions which all the Churches of the Communion require in order to live together in harmony and unity." The Primates formed the Anglican Consultative Legal Advisors' Network and asked the group to produce a statement of the principles of canon law common to the churches.

"Impaired Communion" and *The Windsor Report*
The threatened fracturing of the Anglican Communion became real on November 20, 2003 when

the House of Bishops of the Church of the Province of Uganda passed the following resolution:

> The Church of the Province of Uganda cuts her relationship and Communion with the Episcopal Church of the United States of America . . . We are grieved by the continued unbiblical actions of the leadership of [TEC] that has led to its separation from a majority of the Anglican Communion.

On December 2, 2003, the Province of South East Asia became the second Province to break communion with TEC as a result of the Robinson Consecration, stating that the "purported consecration [of Gene Robinson] was a flagrant disregard of the fundamental teachings of the Bible and the long established doctrines of the Church." By 2006, 22 of the 38 Provinces of the Anglican Communion had declared themselves to be in "broken" or "impaired" communion with TEC.

The Akron Confirmations

For the clergy of the orthodox TEC parishes, 2004 was a year of waiting because the Eames Commission did not issue its report until October. However, several other noteworthy events occurred earlier in 2004. First, in March 2004, over 800 orthodox Episcopalians gathered at a church in Akron, Ohio, for the confirmation of 110 people by five retired Episcopal bishops, including the Rt. Rev. FitzSimmons Allison, the retired Bishop of the Diocese of South Carolina and the Rt. Rev. Alex Dickson, the retired Bishop of West Tennessee.

The "Akron Confirmations" were noteworthy because they were held without the knowledge and consent of the diocesan bishop, the Rt. Rev. J. Clark Crew. Territorial lines had been crossed in blatant disregard of Anglican *canon law* and centuries of tradition. When asked why he participated in these confirmations, Bishop Allison stated: "I was given a choice between obeying the Scriptures or obeying the Canons. To have chosen the Canons would have been idolatry."

The Primates of the Global South Met in Nairobi in April 2004

The second significant event in 2004 occurred on April 15-16, when the Primates of the Global South, representing 18 Provinces with a combined membership of over 55 million Anglicans, met together in Nairobi under the leadership of the Most Rev. Dr. Peter Akinola, the Primate of Nigeria. These Primates of the Global South reaffirmed their commitment to: (1) the historic and apostolic Christian faith in the Holy Scriptures once delivered to the Saints, (2) the 1998 Lambeth Resolution on human sexuality, and (3) the unanimously agreed upon statement of the Primates on October 16, 2003. The Primates from the Global South then unanimously approved the following suggestions to the Eames Commission:

1. The Commission should include in its report a specific call to [TEC] to repent; revoking and rescinding their action regarding the consecration of Gene Robinson as a Bishop in the Church of God.
2. Should [TEC] not comply within three months, the Archbishop of Canterbury and the Primates should take appropriate disciplinary action which should include the suspension and ultimate expulsion of [TEC] from fellowship and membership of the Anglican Communion.

3. Recognition and full Episcopal and pastoral oversight should be given by the Archbishop of Canterbury and the Primates to the dioceses, parishes and laity within [TEC] who continue to uphold the historic faith and order of the Anglican Communion.

Finally, on October 22, 2004, the Eames Commission released its long awaited report, *The Windsor Report,* that contained the Commission's recommendations for maintaining and strengthening unity in the Anglican Communion. The 93 page report made four specific recommendations:

1. A moratorium on developing rites for same-sex blessings.
2. A moratorium on the election and consecration of additional non-celibate homosexual persons.
3. The bishops from the Global South should refrain from offering oversight to any additional [TEC] congregations.
4. Provinces of the Anglican Communion should adopt as a part of their canon law provisions dealing with unity in the communion and then sign a covenant agreeing to maintain unity within the Anglican Communion.

The Windsor Report received mixed reviews. The Primates from the Global South had called for "repentance" on the part of TEC. However, the report had recommended that the TEC bishops who had participated in Robinson's consecration express their "deep regret" for the pain and divisiveness that the consecration had caused within the Anglican Communion. The Most Rev. Peter Akinola, the Primate of Nigeria and chairman of the Council of Anglican Provinces in Africa (CAPA), made the following statement concerning the report:

> The report fails to confront the reality that a small, economically privileged group of people has sought to subvert the Christian faith and impose their new and false doctrine on the wider community of faithful believers. . . .Where are the words of "deep regret" for the impact of TEC's actions upon the Global South and our missionary efforts? We have been asked to express regret for our actions and to affirm our desire to remain in communion. How patronizing!

The Windsor Report also contained a proposed "Anglican Covenant" that had been drafted by Professor Doe. The report suggested that each province of the Anglican Communion adopt the covenant and include it in their respective "constitutions and canons." According to Professor Doe:

> The Anglican Communion is understood as a fellowship of autonomous churches, each with its own legal system, in communion with the See of Canterbury. There is no body, at the global level, competent to make decisions binding on churches: they are held together by non-juridical bonds of affection.

Thus, the Eames Commission concluded in *The Windsor Report* that the case for the adoption of an Anglican Covenant was overwhelming in order to: (a) strengthen the bonds of unity between the churches; (b) to articulate what to-date has been assumed; and (c) to make explicit and forceful the loyalty and bonds of affection which govern the relationships between the churches of the Communion.

When asked about the prospects of TEC adopting the proposed Anglican covenant, TEC Presiding Bishop Frank Griswold replied evasively: "This notion will need to be studied with particular care." However, the House of Bishops of TEC did hold a special meeting to consider the other recommendations of *The Windsor Report*. The Eames Commission had recommended a moratorium on the elections and consecration of additional non-celibate homosexual persons. However, the revisionist bishops within TEC felt that such a moratorium would be discriminatory against homosexual candidates. Therefore, they agreed to a moratorium on the election of *all* bishops until the next TEC General Convention in 2006.

Following the 2006 TEC General Convention, the Number of Breakaway Anglican Churches Increased Dramatically

The number of Breakaway Anglican Churches increased dramatically during 2006. For example, on February 2, 2006, St. Anne's Church in Oceanside, California became the second Episcopal congregation in two months to break away from the Episcopal Diocese of San Diego; and on February 8, 2006, Church of Holy Spirit in Ashburn, Virginia became the second Episcopal congregation to sever its ties from the Diocese of Virginia. These congregations sought "alternative episcopal oversight" from Bishops in Bolivia and Uganda respectively.

The 75th TEC General Convention convened on June 13, 2006 in Columbus, Ohio. On the evening of June 14, a public hearing was held to receive input concerning the *Windsor Report*. More than 1,000 people packed the Hyatt Regency Ballroom for the two-and-a-half hour hearing. Bishop Robert Duncan, representing the Network, offered the following testimony:

> I believe, with the greatest of heartbreak and sadness, that the day has arrived where those who have chosen The Episcopal Church because of its catholic and evangelical reliability, and those who have chosen The Episcopal Church for its revolutionary character, can no longer be held together. For which Episcopal Church will the Committee, and then this Convention, decide? The future in Communion rests only with the former of the two. It cannot be both ways into the future.

Also, on June 18, 2006, the General Convention elected Katherine Jefferts Schori, Bishop of Nevada, as its first female presiding bishop. Jefferts Schori had voted in favor of Gene Robinson's consecration in 2003 and was described by some as a "woman of inclusion."

The Diocese of Fort Worth Severed All Ties with TEC

Following Jefferts Schori's election, the Bishop and Standing Committee of the Diocese of Fort Worth, Texas voted unanimously to seek "alternative *primatial* oversight" (APO). Over one hundred individual *parishes* had sought "alternative *episcopal* oversight" since Gene Robinson's consecration in 2003; however, the Diocese of Fort Worth became the first entire *diocese* to do so.

At the 2006 TEC Convention, a vote was taken on Resolution A161 which would have effected a moratorium on the consecration of homosexual bishops and the blessing of same sex unions as mandated by the *Windsor Report*; however, Resolution A161 failed to pass. As a result, the alienation of TEC from the Anglican Communion was assured. However, on the last day of the convention, at the insistence of Presiding Bishop Griswold, both the House of Deputies and the House of Bishops passed Resolution B033 that provided in part:

> Resolved that the 75th General Convention receive and embrace the *Windsor Report's* invitation to engage in a process of healing and reconciliation; and be it further Resolved that this Convention call upon Standing Committees and bishops to exercise restraint by not consenting to the consecration of any candidate to the episcopate whose manner of life presents a challenge to the wider church and will lead to further strains on communion.

The words, "moratorium on the consecration of homosexuals," and "prohibition of the blessing of same sex unions" were conspicuously absent from Resolution B033. Nevertheless, the Convention had responded to the *Windsor Report.*

Bishop Duncan Acknowledged that the "Inside Strategy" Had Failed

Following the General Convention, Bishop Robert Duncan, Moderator of the Network, issued a pastoral letter that tacitly acknowledged that the "inside strategy" had failed. He stated:

It is with sadness, but also with anticipation, that I write to you now that the General Convention of The Episcopal Church has provided clarity for which we have long prayed. By almost every assessment, the General Convention has embraced the course of "walking apart". . . . Even before the close of the Convention, Network and Windsor Bishops began disassociating themselves from the inadequate "Windsor Resolution," and thus far, one Network diocese [the Diocese of Fort Worth, Texas] has formally requested alternative primatial oversight.

Fourteen other TEC bishops, including Bishop Edward Salmon of the Diocese of South Carolina and Bishop FitzSimmons Allison, retired Bishop of the Diocese of South Carolina, signed a letter that declared that the Convention's responses to the *Windsor Report* were "clearly and simply inadequate."

Following the TEC General Convention, several other dioceses joined Fort Worth in asking for alternative primatial oversight: Central Florida; Dallas; Pittsburgh; San Joaquin (Fresno, California); Northern Indiana; and South Carolina. These dioceses said that they did not intend to leave TEC, but they wanted to disassociate themselves from the decisions made at the General Convention, especially the General Convention's response to the *Windsor Report.*

Christ Church Plano, Truro Church, and The Falls Church Leave TEC

In addition to the four dioceses that had requested alternative primatial oversight following the 2006 TEC General Convention, three of the oldest and largest TEC parishes voted to sever their ties with TEC: Christ Church, Plano in the Diocese of Dallas; and Truro

Church, Fairfax and The Falls Church in the Diocese of Virginia. On June 24, 2006, Christ Church, Plano, the largest TEC parish in terms of average Sunday attendance, voted to "disassociate" from TEC and accepted "temporary alternative episcopal oversight" from Bishop Bill Godfrey, the Bishop of Peru.

On June 28, 2006, the Primate of All Nigeria (Anglican Communion), the Most Rev. Peter Akinola, announced the election of new Bishops in the Church of Nigeria. Among the bishops elected was the Rev. Canon Martyn Minns, the former rector of Truro Church in Virginia. Minns was consecrated in July 2006 as Bishop for the missionary initiative of the Church of Nigeria called the Convocation of Anglican Churches in North America (CANA).

On November 12-13, 2006, the Vestries of Truro Church and The Falls Church, with a combined membership of 5,200, recommended to their respective congregations that they "disaffiliate" from TEC and affiliate with a newly formed Convocation of Anglicans in North America (CANA) under the oversight of Bishop Martyn Minns.

By December 31, 2006, 11 parishes in Virginia, representing 25 percent of the members in the Diocese of Virginia, had voted to breakaway from TEC. Over 20 parishes in the Diocese of Florida also were making plans to breakaway from TEC. Over 10,000 Episcopalians left TEC in 2006.

Rumors became rampant that the creation of a new orthodox "structure" was imminent, and some speculated that CANA would be the core of that structure. In response, the Secretary General of the Anglican Communion issued a formal statement to the contrary stating that CANA was a "mission" of the Church of Nigeria and "not a branch of the Anglican Communion as such." The statement concluded by adding that the Archbishop of Canterbury had not "indicated any support for its establishment" as a separate structure or province.

The Global South Bishops Gathered in Kigali in September 2006 and Called For a Separate "Ecclesiastical Structure"

On September 19, 2006, three months after the TEC General Convention, 25 Anglican Archbishops and other leaders from Africa, Asia, and Latin America attended a meeting of the Global South primates and leaders in Kigali, Rwanda. The delegates issued a statement that contained the following conclusions:

1. We recognize that because of the ongoing conflict in the Communion many people have lost hope that we will come to any resolution in the foreseeable future. We are grateful therefore, that one sign of promise is the widespread support for the development of an Anglican Covenant. We are delighted to affirm the extraordinary progress made by the Global South task group on developing an Anglican Covenant.

2. We deeply regret that, at its most recent General Convention, The Episcopal Church gave no clear embrace of the minimal recommendations of the Windsor Report. We observe that a number of the resolutions adopted by the Convention were actually contrary to the Windsor Report.

3. We are, however, greatly encouraged by the continued faithfulness of the Network Dioceses and all of the other congregations and communities of faithful Anglicans in North America. We are also pleased by the emergence of a wider circle of "Windsor Dioceses" and urge all of them to walk more closely

together and deliberately work towards the unity that Christ enjoins.

4. After a great deal of prayer and deliberation, and in order to support these faithful Anglican diocese and parishes, we have come to agreement on the following actions:

a. We have asked the Global South Steering Committee to meet with the leadership of the dioceses requesting Alternative Primatial Oversight, in consultation with the Archbishop of Canterbury, the Network and the Windsor Dioceses, to investigate their appeal in greater detail and to develop a proposal identifying the ways by which the requested Primatial Oversight can be adequately provided.

b. We are convinced that the time has now come to take initial steps towards the formation of what will be recognized as a separate "ecclesiastical structure" of the Anglican Communion in the USA. We have asked the Global South Steering Committee to develop such a proposal in consultation with the appropriate instruments of unity of the Communion.

The Primates of the Anglican Communion Met in Tanzania in February 2007

In early 2007, the stage was set for the implementation of a "new structure" for the orthodox dioceses and parishes in the United States and Canada. This critical issue would face the Primates of the Anglican Communion as they gathered for their annual meeting February 14-19, 2007 in Tanzania.

Reporters who attended the Primates' meeting in Tanzania found security tight. They were not allowed to attend any actual meetings of the Primates, and the news that they reported came from brief interviews with Primates that they encountered in the courtyard going to and from the sessions.

In her opening address to the Primates, TEC Presiding Bishop Jefferts Schori announced boastfully to the Primates that the "Episcopal Church of the United States" (ECUSA) had changed its name to "The Episcopal Church" (TEC) in order to better reflect its international constituency. Several of the other thirty-seven provinces of the Anglican Communion included "Episcopal" in their names, including the Episcopal Church of Rwanda.

The Primates from these Provinces were astounded by the unmitigated gall of the Presiding Bishop's claim that ECUSA was now "The" Episcopal Church. In direct response to this affront, at its next House of Bishops meeting, the Episcopal Church of Rwanda changed its name to the "Anglican" Church of Rwanda.

To the shock and dismay of the Global South Primates who attended the meeting of the Primates in Tanzania, discussion of a "separate ecclesiastical structure" was not placed on the agenda, and the issue was not even addressed by the Primates. Rather, discussion centered around "The Windsor Report," "Millennium Development Goals," and the future relationship between TEC and the wider Anglican Communion. The Archbishop of Canterbury held the final press conference.

The Archbishop of Canterbury's Remarks at the Final Press Conference of the Anglican Primates' Meeting in Tanzania.

On February 20, 2007, the Archbishop of Canterbury told reporters that the business of following through with the recommendations of The Windsor Report covered "a great deal of our business and it touches on what we've called the listening process. . . ." He added the following comment that astounded both the reporters and the Global South Primates:

> In short, the feeling of the meeting as a whole was that the response of the General Convention of The Episcopal Church to the recommendations of the Windsor report—a response made at General Convention last year—represented some steps in a very encouraging direction but did not yet represent a situation in which we could say "business as usual."

> The response of The Episcopal Church, while not wholly clear, represented a willingness to engage with the Communion and awareness of the cost of difficulty that decisions have generated, so our first question is "how do we best engage with that willingness?" How do we work with the stream of desire to remain with the Communion?

> The second factor is the very substantial group of bishops and others within The Episcopal Church, perhaps amounting to nearly one quarter of the Bishops, who have spelled out not only their willingness to abide by the Windsor Report in all its aspects, but to provide a carefully worked-through system of pastoral oversight for those in The Episcopal Church who are not content with the decisions of General Convention.

Once again, "the Americans had paid, the Africans had prayed, and the English had written up the resolutions." Rather than the "separate ecclesiastical structure" that the Global South Primates had requested, they received "a carefully worked-through system of pastoral oversight." Rather than returning home with a thirty-ninth province, Bob Duncan, an invited guest to the gathering, returned home from Tanzania with virtually nothing substantive to report the members of The Network and CANA.

8

CAPA and GAFCON

<u>The Council of Anglican Provinces of Africa (CAPA)</u>
<u>October 2-5, 2007</u>

E very five years, the Anglican Archbishops of Africa gather for a meeting to update each other on the affairs of their respective provinces. At the meeting, each Archbishop is given the opportunity to report on his province's progress in four areas:

1. Evangelism
2. Poverty
3. AIDS
4. Water

Ellis Brust, the CEO of The Anglican Mission, Cynthia Brust, the Public Affairs Officer of The Anglican Mission, Kevin Donlon, the Canon of Ecclesiastical Affairs of The Anglican Mission, and Ross Lindsay represented The Anglican Mission at the October 2007 CAPA meeting. Bishop Martyn Minns represented CANA and the ACN.

The Primates were supposed to meet on the evening before the conference began in order to finalize the agenda, and Archbishop Kolini had arranged for Kevin Donlon and Ross Lindsay to present the case for calling a "church council" to deal with TEC and the related issues that were fracturing the wider Anglican Communion at that meeting. However, Archbishop Akinola did not attend the meeting, so it was cancelled. Ellis and Cynthia Brust had arrived in Mauritius a day early and reported that they had seen Akinola at the Hilton Resort on the other side of the island earlier that afternoon.

The next morning Archbishop Akinola checked into to the far less luxurious hotel where the conference was being held, and his room adjoined Kevin Donlon's. Akinola literally bumped into Kevin Donlon in the hall enroute to the first plenary session. Akinola recognized Donlon because the two of them had served on a committee to write a Catechism for the Anglican Communion. The next day, Akinola introduced Donlon to the delegates as the "Chief Catechist" of the Anglican Communion.

During the plenary sessions, one by one, the Archbishops presented their reports. The report of Archbishop Henry Orombi of Uganda was singularly impressive. Orombi not only reported astounding numbers of new church plants and new Christians in Uganda, but he also reported that the Anglican Church of Uganda had taken over the public education system for the province including the university whose name had been changed to Uganda Christian University. Reports from the other archbishops were not as encouraging.

Kevin Donlon and Ross Lindsay were able to meet privately with several of the archbishops to discuss Donlon's proposal for calling a "church council."

Archbishop Orombi politely informed Donlon and Lindsay that Uganda had been willing to provide "temporary" episcopal oversight for several congregations that had chosen to leave TEC, but that neither he nor the Province of Uganda had the time nor the money to pursue the matter further because it needed to devote its resources to larger issues at home like evangelism, poverty, AIDS, and water. Orombi was true to his word. Within hours after the ACNA was legally chartered in 2009, Orombi sent an email transferring all the TEC churches under his oversight to the ACNA.

At the last session of the CAPA conference, Bishop Martyn Minns projected a draft of the final communiqué onto a screen. Apparently, Minns and Archbishop Akinola had drafted the communique well in advance of the conference because several of the points in the statement had not been discussed during the conference. Several delegates suggested substantive changes to the communiqué, and some minor changes were made. However, the final communiqué was the work of Minns and Akinola, not of the delegates to CAPA 2007.

This time, the delegates from The Anglican Mission, rather than Bob Duncan, returned home empty handed. Very few of the archbishops, other than Archbishop Emmanuel Kolini of Rwanda, had supported Kevin Donlon's call for a "church council."

GAFCON: June 2008

Undaunted by the rebuff that they had received at the Primates' meeting in Tanzania, Bob Duncan, The ACN, and CANA decided to raise the ante. They called for a "Global Anglican Future Conference" (GAFCON) to be held in Jerusalem in June of 2008.

The Global Anglican Future Conference (GAFCON) was held in Jerusalem from June 22-29, 2008. 1,148 lay and clergy participants, including 291 bishops representing millions of faithful Anglican Christians, attended the conference. According to the conference promoters, "GAFCON was not just a moment in time, but a movement in the Spirit;" and the conference resolved to:

- launch the GAFCON movement as a fellowship of confessing Anglicans
- publish the Jerusalem Declaration as the basis of the fellowship
- encourage the GAFCON Primates' Council.

GAFCON was full of surprises. First, some of those attending the conference could not get visas into Israel, so a "pre-conference" meeting was arranged in Egypt. Chuck Murphy and Kevin Donlon traveled to Egypt to attend this pre-conference, but they learned, after waiting around all day for the meeting to begin, that Archbishop Akinola had been denied entrance into the country, so the pre-conference had been cancelled. Archbishop Akinola had asserted diplomatic privilege when he arrived at the airport in Egypt with no visa, but the Egyptian immigration officials refused to allow him into the country because he had not applied for a visa.

The next surprise was the revelation to the delegates from the United States that Bob Duncan, their leader, would not be attending the conference. The delegates were dismayed when they learned that the leader of their movement, who had been intimately involved in arranging the dates and minute details of the conference, suddenly had a "personal conflict" that prevented him from attending.

The final surprise occurred when Kevin Donlon, the Canon for Ecclesiastical Affairs for The Anglican Mission was removed from the "theological resource committee" for GAFCON. Donlon had been appointed to the committee by Archbishop Kolini; however, the GAFCON organizers had questioned Donlon's credentials and removed him from the committee. Donlon has a Ph.D. in Church History from Oxford and an L.L.M. in Canon Law from Cardiff Law School, but the GAFCON organizers said that since he had not published anything, he could not serve on the committee. A power struggle ensued, but Kolini prevailed and Donlon was placed back on the committee.

The next day at a "town hall meeting" for the delegates from the United States and Canada, Kevin Donlon informed the delegates that they were not going home with a province. Many of the delegates had been led to believe that the purpose of GAFCON was to create a separate ecclesiastical structure for North American Anglicans. Donlon, an astute canon lawyer, suggested to the delegates that they could form a new Anglican "church" if they wished, but only a majority of the Primates of the wider Anglican Communion could create and recognize a thirty-ninth "province"—not a majority of the "GAFCON Primates."

The delegates from The ACN and CANA were distraught. Bishop John Guernsey telephoned Bob Duncan and thrust his phone into Kevin Donlon's face. "Bishop Duncan wants a word with you," Guernsey screamed. Duncan chastised Donlon for telling the delegates that the GAFCON Primates could not send them home with a "province." A year later at the first Assembly of the ACNA in Toronto, Bob Duncan demanded that Donlon "take his seat" after Donlon raised a point of order from the floor. Donlon replied indignantly: "I have no dog in this fight. I am just telling you what is canonically correct, and what is not. Any new ecclesiastical structure must be consistent with canon law, or it will not be recognized by the Archbishop of Canterbury and the Primates."

While pursuing his L.L.M. in Canon Law at the Centre of Law and Religion at Cardiff Law School, Donlon had studied under Norman Doe, the advisor to the Archbishop of Canterbury; and he had met with John Rees, the Chancellor for the Archbishop of Canterbury; and Mark Hill, the Editor of The Ecclesiastical Law Journal. Donlon not only knew what was canonically correct, he knew personally the advisors to the Archbishop of Canterbury who would ultimately decide when and if the ACNA would be recognized as a province. However, Bob Duncan and his advisors, including the three chancellors of ACNA (none of whom had degrees in canon law), paid little heed to Donlon's suggestions. Donlon and Lindsay had also offered their legal services to Duncan and the Diocese of Pittsburgh and to the breakaway churches in Virginia during their church property litigation. Duncan and the Virginia breakaway churches declined their offer of assistance. And subsequently, the courts ruled against Duncan and ACNA and awarded the property of the Diocese of Pittsburgh to TEC. The Supreme Court of Virginia also ruled against the Virginia breakaway churches and in favor of TEC holding that a confederate statute that the Virginia breakaway churches had relied upon was unconstitutional. The issue of the validity of the Dennis Canon in Virginia was still on appeal to the Virginia Supreme Court in mid 2011.

Archbishop Kolini and Bishop Nazir-Ali Called for a Church Council

Two competing forces were at work at GAFCON: 1) those who were trying to restore the "faith" that was given to the Saints and 2) those who were trying to preserve the "order" that was given to the Saints. Since its inception, the purpose of the canon law had been to preserve "order" within the church. Kevin Donlon, Archbishop Kolini, and Church of England Bishop Michael Nazir-Ali maintained throughout the conference that nothing less than a "chuch council" could restore "faith" and "order" to the church. However, their recommendations fell on deaf ears.

So, GAFCON ended precisely as Kevin Donlon had predicted that it would. Once again, "The Americans had paid, the Africans had prayed, and the English had written the communiqué." The GAFCON Communiqué included the following statements:

> The Anglican Communion, present in six continents, is well positioned to address this challenge [from TEC], but currently it is divided and distracted. The Global Anglican Future Conference has emerged in response to a crisis within the Anglican Communion, a crisis involving three undeniable facts concerning world Anglicanism.

> The first fact is the acceptance and promotion within the provinces of the Anglican Communion of a different "gospel" that is contrary to the apostolic gospel.

> The second fact is the declaration by provincial bodies in the Global South that they are out of communion with bishops and churches that promote this

false gospel. These declarations have resulted in a realignment whereby faithful Anglican Christians have left existing territorial parishes, dioceses and provinces in certain Western churches and become members of other dioceses and provinces, all within the Anglican Communion.

The third fact is the manifest failure of the Communion Instruments to exercise discipline in the face of overt heterodoxy. The Episcopal Church USA [TEC] and the Anglican Church of Canada, in proclaiming this false gospel, have consistently defied the 1998 Lambeth statement of biblical moral principle (Resolution 1.10). Despite numerous meetings and reports to and from the "Instruments of Unity," no effective action has been taken, and the bishops of these unrepentant churches are welcomed to Lambeth 2008.

The communiqué also included "The Jerusalem Declaration" that contained fourteen points of agreement. The thirteenth was the most salient:

13. We reject the authority of those churches and leaders who have denied the orthodox faith in word or deed. We pray for them and call on them to repent and return to the Lord.

Like *The Windsor Report* that preceded it, "The Jerusalem Declaration" called for TEC "to repent and return to the Lord." It did not create or even call for a 39th province for the theologically conservative Anglicans in the United States and Canada.

9

The CONVOCATION OF ACNA and the FOURTH GLOBAL SOUTH ENCOUNTER IN SINGAPORE

The Convocation of the Anglican Church in North America: June 2009

R eeling from yet another disappointment at GAFCON, Bob Duncan, the ACN, and CANA decided to take matters into their own hands. They called for the creation of the Anglican Church of North America (the ACNA) and scheduled an inaugural assembly in Fort Worth, Texas for June 2009.

On June 22, 2009, exactly one year after GAFCON had convened, the Convocation of the Anglican Church in North America began in Bedford, Texas, a suburb of Fort Worth. The opening worship service was filled with pomp and circumstance. The priests in charge were older, "high-church" Anglo-Catholics, but the majority of the delegates were younger, "low-church" Anglicans who were more accustomed to worship leaders and Christian rock bands than "smells and bells" during

Morning Prayer. Following the service, many of the delegates grumbled in the parking lot about the number of "Anglo-Catholics" in attendance and in control of the conference.

Nevertheless, after two days of seemingly endless debate, the proposed ACNA Constitution was ratified on June 23, 2009 at 4:23 p.m. The ACNA was legally constituted. The debate had been punctuated by "mission minutes" that were the highlight of the first two days of the conference.

During one of these "mission minutes," CANA Bishop Bena, a retired Marine, told the delegates about a "healing ministry" to "wounded warriors" that he and several other CANA priests had initiated. Bishop Bena asked for a show of hands from the 1,200 delegates of those who had witnessed an actual physical healing following intercessory prayer. To the surprise of many, a majority of the delegates raised their hands.

The second night of the Convocation, Trinity School for Ministry in Pittsburgh (TSM), the last bastion of evangelicalism within TEC, hosted a dinner for alumni at a nearby Texas steakhouse. The overflow crowd spilled over into several dining rooms. Many of the theologically conservative delegates to the ACNA Convocation were Trinity alumni which explained the overwhelming response to Bishop Bena's question about healing. The power of prayer and especially intercessory and healing prayer were taught at Trinity. Unlike the students at some of the other TEC seminaries, Trinity students were taught to expect the living God to respond to healing prayer.

After the Constitution and Canons had been officially adopted, Bob Duncan reported on the work of the College of Bishops the previous week. According to Duncan, the bishops had completed the election of eight bishops for several dioceses and had officially elected him as the "Archbishop-designate" of the Anglican Church in North America. Bob Duncan then read an email from Ugandan Archbishop Henry Orombi congratulating the delegates on the organization of the ACNA and transferring the American and Canadian churches that were under his oversight to the newly created ACNA.

Finally, Bob Duncan reported that the Anglican Church in North America had united some 100,000 Anglicans in 700 parishes into a single church. The jurisdictions that had joined together to form the 28 dioceses and dioceses-in-formation of the Anglican Church in North America were: the dioceses of Fort Worth, Pittsburgh, Quincy, and San Joaquin; the Anglican Mission in the Americas; the Convocation of Anglicans in North America; the Anglican Network in Canada; the Anglican Coalition in Canada; the Reformed Episcopal Church; and the missionary initiatives of Kenya, Uganda, and South America's Southern Cone. Additionally, the American Anglican Council (the AAC) and Forward in Faith North America (FiFNA) were founding organizations.

Rick Warren Spoke and Bob Duncan was Enthroned

Rick Warren, the pastor of Saddleback Church in California, was the keynote speaker for the conference. Warren told the delegates that he had only accepted two speaking engagements that year and the Convocation of ACNA was one of them to which the crowd responded with thunderous applause. Warren reiterated comments that he had made at the Hope and a Future Conference in Pittsburgh five years earlier that a "new reformation" had begun within the church, and that theologically conservative Anglicans, especially those in the Global South and in North America, would play a key role in this reformation.

The last night of the conference, a service of enthronement was held at Christ Church, Plano where Bob Duncan was officially installed as the Archbishop of the ACNA. This service was also full of pomp and circumstance; however, the "smells and bells" were absent. The lower church Anglicans were much more comfortable in Dave Roseberry's sanctuary at Plano than they had been at the Cathedral in Bedford. However, many were surprised that Bob Duncan preached at his own coronation.

In the Anglican tradition, at least two other bishops participate in the consecration of a new bishop, and one of those bishops preaches following the installation and delivers "the charge" to the new bishop. As he was prone to do, Bob Duncan ignored the tradition and canon law. He had waited a long time for this moment, and he basked in its glory as he entered the pulpit to preach his first sermon as the Archbishop of ACNA.

The Anglican Mission was a "founding organization" of the ACNA. However, following ACNA's first "Assembly" that was held in Toronto in December 2009, a review of the canons of the Anglican Church of Rwanda by Kevin Donlon revealed that The Anglican Mission could not be canonically resident in both the Anglican Church of Rwanda and in ACNA. Therefore, in early 2010, The Anglican Mission opted to remain a missionary outreach of, and canonically resident in, the Anglican Church of Rwanda. The Anglican Mission remained a "ministry partner" with ACNA, but it was no longer a voting member of the new church.

Therefore, five years after the Hope and a Future Conference in Pittsburgh and one year after GAFCON in Jerusalem, The Anglican Church in North America had been duly constituted. An "ecclesiastical structure" for theologically conservative Anglicans finally existed in North America. The ACNA was legally a "church," but it had yet to be recognized by the Primates as the thirty-ninth "province" of the wider Anglican Communion.

Could the Global South Primates bring enough pressure to bear upon the Archbishop of Canterbury and the other Primates to recognize ACNA as a thirty-ninth province? Only time would tell, but Bob Duncan and the leaders of the ACNA had high hopes that the "Fourth Global South Encounter" to be held in Singapore in April 2010 would be the next step in that process.

The Fourth Global South Encounter: Singapore, April 2010

On Monday, April 19, 2010, 130 primates, bishops, clergy, senior lay leaders, associates and observers arrived for "The Fourth Trumpet," a five-day "Encounter," in Singapore. Many of the delegates, including Ugandan Primate Henry Orombi, had been stranded or delayed in airports for several days after ash from a volcanic eruption in Iceland had grounded flights all across Europe.

Chuck and Margaret Murphy flew west through California and arrived in Singapore on time. However, Kevin Donlon and Susan Grayson, Chuck Murphy's chief of staff, were scheduled to fly east through Frankfurt. After spending twelve hours in New York City's JFK airport, they were told that all flights to Europe had been cancelled. Several hours later they were re-routed through Anchorage, Alaska and Tiawan. Donlon and Grayson finally arrived in Singapore the next day safely but exhausted. Ross Lindsay, who was supposed to accompany Donlon and Grayson, was unable to book a flight going either West or East to Singapore, so he missed the conference entirely.

The stated purpose of the Encounter was to build upon the ecclesiological vision of the "One Holy, Catholic and Apostolic Church of Jesus Christ" that was shared at the previous "Encounter" at El-ein-Suknah, Egypt in 2005. The theme of this Fourth Encounter was: "The Gospel of Jesus Christ—Covenant for the People; Light for the Nations," and the mission statement was: "To Recover, Reform, Revitalize, and Restore Ourselves as an Anglican Covenantal Community for Mission and Ministry in Jesus Christ."

Chuck Murphy and Kevin Donlon represented The Anglican Mission at the Encounter, and Archbishop Emmanuel Kolini represented the Anglican Church of Rwanda. The agenda called for discussion and presumably for the adoption of the "Anglican Covenant" that had been proposed by "The Windsor Report" and revised by Archbishop Drexel Gomez of the West Indies and several other representatives from the Global South. However, to the chagrin of the conference organizers, the adoption of the Covenant received very little traction from the delegates.

In an effort to bring attention to the more critical issues at hand, Archbishop Emmanuel Kolini of Rwanda, with the assistance of Kevin Donlon, proposed to the delegates that a "church council" be called to deal with the critical issues that were confronting the wider Anglican Communion. David Virtue and the other reporters that attended the Encounter seized upon the idea to call a church council as a fresh and innovative approach to break the impasse that had existed for years between the Primates of the Provinces in the Global South and the Archbishop of Canterbury and the other Primates of the wider Anglican Communion. (Kolini's and Donlon's proposal is reproduced as Appendix 1)

Kolini's proposal to call a church council gained more consensus than the proposal to adopt the covenant. However, at the end of the day, the English wrote the final communiqué; and neither the "covenant" nor the "call for a church council," made it into the press release that stated in part:

> We were grateful for the gracious guidance of the Holy Spirit. A total of 130 delegates from 20 provinces in the Global South (comprising Africa, West Indies, Asia and South America) gathered together. We represented the vast majority of the active membership of the Anglican Communion.

> We continue to grieve over the life of The Episcopal Church USA [TEC] and the Anglican Church of Canada and all those churches that have rejected the Way of the Lord as expressed in Holy Scripture These churches continue in their defiance as they set themselves on a course that contradicts the plain teaching of the Holy Scriptures on matters so fundamental that they affect the very salvation of those involved. Such actions violate the integrity of the Gospel, the Communion and our Christian witness to the rest of the world. In the face of this we dare not remain silent and must respond with appropriate action.

> We uphold the courageous actions taken by Archbishops Mouneer Anis (Jerusalem and the Middle East), Henry Orombi (Uganda) and Ian Ernest (Indian Ocean) and are encouraged by their decision not to participate in meetings of the various

Instruments of Communion at which representatives of The Episcopal Church USA and the Anglican Church of Canada are present. We understand their actions to be in protest of the failure to correct the ongoing crisis situation.

In light of the above, this Fourth South-to-South Encounter encourages our various Provinces to reconsider their communion relationships with The Episcopal Church USA and the Anglican Church of Canada until it becomes clear that there is genuine repentance.

Global South leaders have been in the forefront of the development of the "Anglican Covenant" that seeks to articulate the essential elements of our faith together with means by which we might exercise meaningful and loving discipline for those who depart from the "faith once for all delivered to the saints." We are currently reviewing the proposed Covenant to find ways to strengthen it in order for it to fulfill its purpose.

The Fourth Encounter may have been in Singapore, but the final communiqué had that English ring to it. No mention was made of Archbishop Kolini's call for a "church council", nor was any mention made of the "separate ecclesiastical structure" that had been requested by the ACNA. Thus, both The Anglican Mission and the ACNA came home from Singapore empty-handed. Upon returning home, Chuck Murphy remarked that the Fourth Encounter more closely resembled a TEC General Convention, than a Global South gathering.

Archbishop Tay of South East Asia had retired in 2008. Archbishop Akinola of Nigeria had retired in

2009, and Archbishop Kolini was retiring in 2010. The stalwarts of the theologically conservative "old guard" were passing their batons to a much younger and more liberal cadre of leaders. Archbishop Henry Luke Orombi of Uganda was the last of the vanguard, the last of the bold and radical Global South bishops who had heard the cry of the theologically conservative Anglicans in North America and had responded in force. Was Singapore 2010 a theological "tipping point" for the Global South? Only time would tell.

10

CANONICAL CONUNDRUMS: THE JURIDICAL CONTEXTS IN WHICH THE BREAKAWAY ANGLICAN CHURCHES EMERGED

The preceding chapters have highlighted the political contexts in which the breakaway Anglican churches emerged. Many of the breakaway churches and orthodox dioceses had cited the Robinson Consecration and the election of Katherine Jefferts Schori as the Presiding Bishop of TEC as reasons for their decision to seek AEO and APO. However, virtually all of the orthodox TEC bishops and priests pointed to the persistent efforts on the part of the revisionist TEC bishops to use, abuse, and amend its *canon law* as the driving force that had produced their irreconcilable differences with TEC. Therefore, the following chapters will discuss the juridical contexts in which the breakaway Anglican churches emerged.

The Canon Law and the Breakaway Anglican Churches
The governing principles of secular bodies typically are called *statutes*. The governing principles of religious bodies typically are called *canons*. When the *canon law* of the church was first codified in the 12th century, it conferred considerable power upon the local *bishops*. One canon lawyer observed astutely: "Each local bishop is a lawgiver and, consequently is a law unto himself." During the early years of the 21st century, many theologically conservative Episcopal congregations and their priests discovered the harsh reality of this observation. All Saints Church in Pawleys Island, South Carolina was one of those local congregations, and Chuck Murphy was one of those priests; but they were not alone. Many others traveled down the same road.

Exclusive Jurisdiction and The Singapore Consecrations
Among other powers, the *canon law* of the church granted to local bishops exclusive ecclesiastical authority within their respective territorial jurisdictions. Other bishops and priests were not allowed to cross these "territorial boundaries" without the consent of the local bishop.

In Singapore, on January 28, 2000, Chuck Murphy, the rector of All Saints Church and John Rodgers, the former dean of Trinity School for Ministry in Pittsburgh, were consecrated as *missionary bishops to the United States* by the Most Rev. Emmanuel Kolini, the Anglican Archbishop of Rwanda and the Most Rev. Moses Tay, the Anglican Archbishop of South East Asia.

In contravention of the *canons*, neither of the Archbishops obtained the required consents from the Presiding Bishop of the Episcopal Church or from the

Archbishop of Canterbury, the titular head of the world-wide Anglican Communion, to cross jurisdictional lines and to consecrate Murphy and Rodgers as missionary bishops to the United States. As a result, the Singapore Consecrations were very controversial.

When the Presiding Bishop of The Episcopal Church, Frank Griswold, learned of the consecrations, he stated: "I am appalled by this irregular action." The Archbishop of Canterbury, George Carey, described the consecrations as "irresponsible and irregular." The Sunday *New York Times* had this to say about the Singapore Consecrations:

> In the pleasant coastal community of Pawleys Island, a place of lush golf resorts and second homes, there is little to evoke Rwanda, a densely populated East African nation . . . . But the two places have a link, a spiritual one which became abruptly apparent in an event that sent shock waves among the world's Anglican churches. The consecrations in Singapore have also reverberated across the Atlantic to England, where the Most Rev. George Carey, Archbishop of Canterbury, declared that he did not recognize them . . . . "There is a crisis of faith and leadership in the American Church," Bishop Murphy said. "Human sexuality issues are but a symptom of the larger problem."

The Rt. Rev. Edward Salmon, Bishop of the Diocese of South Carolina, was given advance notice of the Singapore Consecrations. Salmon's reaction was positive and encouraging. He stated: "A new baby is being born within the Anglican Communion." Yet, several weeks later, Salmon cancelled a diocesan men's conference at St. Michael's Church in Charleston where

Chuck Murphy was to have been the keynote speaker. Presumably, Salmon had received directions to do so from the Presiding Bishop of TEC, Frank Griswold, or his Chancellor, David Booth Beers.

The first shot that was fired in the Civil War between the North and the South in the United States was fired in South Carolina, from Fort Sumter in Charleston Harbor. The first shot in the spiritual war between The Episcopal Church and a handful of theologically conservative Episcopal congregations in the United States also was fired in South Carolina, from All Saints Church in Pawleys Island when the Singapore Consecrations occurred.

The Singapore Consecrations thrust both Chuck Murphy and All Saints Church onto the world stage, but the controversy surrounding the *irregularity* of the consecrations soon gave way to an even more contentious issue, the spurious claim by The Episcopal Church that it owned the property of All Saints Church. The next chapter discusses the canonical conundrums associated with the ownership of church property.

11

THE CANON LAW AND CHURCH PROPERTY

From the 12th century until late in the 20th century, the *canon law* of the church provided that *consecra*ted property (sanctuaries) could not be transferred or encumbered (mortgaged) without the consent of the bishop (or in the case of a Presbyterian Church, the consent of the "Presbytery"). This canon was adopted in the 12th century in order to preserve and protect *consecrated* (sacred) property of local church congregations. In the 21st century, this canon began to be used by revisionist bishops within The Episcopal Church (and the Presbyterian and Methodist churches) to confiscate the church property of theologically conservative congregations that had chosen to withdraw from the denomination, or were contemplating such action.

For example, in 2002, after its rector, Kevin Donlon, had been deposed by TEC Bishop John Lipscomb, St. Mary's Episcopal Church in Tampa, Florida voted to withdraw from TEC. Officials from TEC immediately seized all of St. Mary's property including a $3.6 million sanctuary that had been completed only months prior. The congregation was forced by TEC to vacate the premises and to change its name. St. Mary's successor, the Church of the Resurrection, was welcomed into The Anglican Mission by Archbishop Emmanuel Kolini and Chuck Murphy and has continued to thrive in spite of having had to walk away from all of its property.

In 2003, St. Andrew's Episcopal Church in Morehead City, North Carolina and its successor, All Saints Anglican Church, followed suit. By early 2011, The Anglican Mission had welcomed 252 theologically conservative congregations into the fold, many of which had lost most, and in many cases all, of their church property to TEC.

The average Episcopal congregation in the United States has less than 75 parishioners. These small congregations are no match for the deep pockets of TEC. They simply cannot afford to pay the hundreds of thousands of dollars that All Saints Church paid to defend its church property. Therefore, many theologically conservative congregations, like St. Mary's in Tampa and St. Andrew's in Morehead City walked away from their property, rather than continue to be associated with an apostate church.

The Canon Law Relating to Church Property Changed Drastically in 1979

The original purpose of the property *canon* was to preserve and to protect church sanctuaries, "sacred" buildings, not fellowship halls, Sunday School buildings, playgrounds, and parking lots. At All Saints Church, for example, the sanctuaries occupied less than one-half acre of its 60 acre campus. Therefore, the church property canon (that was adopted by The Episcopal Church in 1868) applied to a small portion of the All Saints Church campus, that is, until 1979.

In 1979, the United States Supreme Court ruled that a local Presbyterian Church in Georgia had to turn over *all* of its property (not just its *sanctuary*) to the national Presbyterian Church after a majority of the members of the congregation voted to withdraw from the denomination. In its opinion, the Supreme Court also suggested that *hierarchical* churches (which it had defined in an earlier case as Episcopal, Presbyterian, and Methodist churches) could better protect their property by amending their *canons* to include language to the effect that every local congregation held its property "in trust" for the national church.

In response to this comment in the Supreme Court decision, the Episcopal, Presbyterian, and Methodist churches promptly amended their *canons* to say that *all* property of local congregations, both real and personal (land, buildings, and cash in the bank including endowments—not just "sacred" property), was held *in trust* for the denomination. The canons stated further that as long as a local congregation remained within the denomination, it could retain title to its church property. However, if for any reason, the congregation chose to withdraw from the denomination, title to *all* of its property, not just its *sanctuaries*, would vest immediately in the denomination.

In The Episcopal Church, the property canon became known as the "Dennis Canon" because Bishop Dennis from New York proposed it for adoption at General Convention of The Episcopal Church in 1979. The Dennis Canon was not on the agenda to be voted on at the convention. Committees typically consider and approve amendments to the Canons and report them out to the delegates for final approval. No committee reported the Dennis Canon out to be voted on. Bishop Dennis simply proposed its adoption on the last day of the convention. The delegates voted on it with no discussion and approved it, having little if any idea what they were voting on.

The Bishop of South Carolina Lays Claim to the All Saints Church Property

On September 11, 2000, amid rumors and speculation that the members of the Vestry of All Saints Church were going to transfer its 60 acre church campus to the Archbishop of Rwanda, the Rt. Rev. Edward L. Salmon, Jr., Bishop of the Episcopal Diocese of South Carolina, filed a "legal notice" in the Georgetown County Courthouse that included the "Dennis Canon" and stated specifically that "all real and personal property held by or for the benefit of All Saints Parish, Waccamaw is held in trust for the Episcopal Diocese of South Carolina and The Episcopal Church."

The Dennis Canon had been adopted by The Episcopal Church in 1979, but it had never been recorded in the respective county court houses in South Carolina. South Carolina is a *res* state which means that legal notices or other legal documents that affect the title to real property must be recorded in the county courthouse in order to be effective. Bishop Salmon's predecessor, the Rt. Rev. FitzSimmons Allison had chosen not to record the Dennis Canon in the county court houses. According to Bishop Allison: "A war would have broken out in Charleston if I had recorded the Dennis Canon in the county courthouse."

The All Saints Church Property Litigation

In response to Bishop Salmon's filing of the "Dennis Canon" in the Georgetown County courthouse, the members of the Vestry of All Saints Church sought a declaratory judgment from the state circuit court that the All Saints Church property was owned by the land trust that had been established by Percival and Anna Pawley in 1745, not by The Episcopal Church.

David Booth Beers, the attorney for TEC, attended the deposition of Chuck Murphy in a meeting room at the airport in Charlotte, North Carolina. Murphy told Beers that the All Saints Church property had been in trust since 1745, long before TEC was established in 1789. Murphy added that the All Saints property could not have been transferred to a trust for TEC in 1979 after the Dennis Canon was adopted because it was already in a trust, and one cannot place a trust on a trust.

Beers was involved heavily in the church property cases of the other breakaway Anglican churches; however, once he learned that the All Saints Church property was held in the Pawley Land Trust, he sent his associate, Heather Anderson, to subsequent depositions, hearings, and trials. Beers did take the deposition of Bishop FitzSimmons Allison by telephone, but he did not set foot in South Carolina again after he learned that the All Saints Church property was held in trust long before the Dennis Canon was adopted. Some believed that Beers had intentionally distanced himself from the All Saints Church case because he knew that the local congregation would ultimately prevail.

In circuit court, Heather Anderson and lawyers for the Diocese of South Carolina argued forcefully that the Pawley Land Trust was no longer valid because the last trustee had died over 200 years ago, because the trustees had had no legal duties after 1767 when the *Parish of All Saints* was established, and because title to the property had vested in The Episcopal Church when the congregation became *dormant* during the Civil War. Both the *canon law* of the church and the *civil law* of the State of South Carolina provided that property of a local congregation that became *dormant* reverted to the larger, national church or denomination.

The Circuit Court Granted Summary Judgment in Favor of All Saints Church

In October 2000, Circuit Court Judge John L. Breeden granted Summary Judgment (a verdict without a trial) in favor of All Saints Church. Judge Breeden ruled that the Pawley Land Trust owned the All Saints Church property and that The Episcopal Church had no interest in the property. TEC and the Diocese appealed the case to the South Carolina Court of Appeals which reversed Judge Breeden, and ordered a full trial to be held on the merits of the case.

After an eight day jury trial in 2007, Circuit Judge Thomas C. Cooper surprised everyone in the courtroom when he dismissed the jury and ruled from the bench that the Pawley Land Trust owned the All Saints Church property and that The Episcopal Church had no interest in the property. The turning point in the trial came when the Chancellor of All Saints Church, Ross Lindsay, a canon lawyer, testified to three things.

Lindsay testified first that title to the All Saints Church property remained in the Trustees of the Pawley Land Trust as it had since the trust was established in 1745. Second, he testified that that prior to 1868, the *canon law* of The Episcopal Church contained no provisions that governed the property of local congregations, and that the *canon* that TEC had adopted in 1868 only applied to *consecrated* property. Finally, Lindsay testified that All Saints Church was not *dormant* during the Civil War. To prove the last point, Lindsay offered into evidence pages of the "Vestry Minute Book" that proved conclusively that meetings of the Vestry and baptisms were held during the period that lawyers for TEC and the Diocese had alleged that All Saints Church was *dormant.*

The Hurricanes of 1893 and the "Vestry Minute Book"
In August and October of 1893, two devastating hurricanes struck coastal South Carolina. According to records contained in the United States Coast Guard Station in Charleston, South Carolina:

The hurricane of 27-28 August 1893 was the worst natural disaster to hit the low country of South Carolina in recorded history. More than one thousand lives were lost and over $10 million of property damage was reported. The storm swept whole families and villages out to sea.

In order to protect the deeds to the *All Saints Church* property, its corporate charter, and its Vestry Minute Book from the impending storm, Dr. Arthur Flagg, the Secretary of the Vestry, stored these important documents in the attic of his home. Sadly, Dr. and Mrs. Flagg and their five young children were drowned by the storm when their home was swept out to sea.
On the day after the storm, another member of the All Saints Church Vestry, J. J. Ward, swam across the inlet to Magnolia Beach (Litchfield Beach today) and discovered the bodies of the Flagg family near the site of their former home. The deeds to the property and the corporate charter were lost forever, but Ward found the Vestry Minute Book half-buried in the sand, soaked with salt water, and torn. However, entries in the Vestry Minute Book from 1830 through the summer of 1893, including the entire period of the Civil War, were legible. These entries proved conclusively that All Saints

Church had not been "dormant" during the period in question, and Judge Cooper ruled accordingly.

The South Carolina Supreme Court Also Ruled in Favor of All Saints Church

TEC and the Diocese of South Carolina appealed Judge Cooper's ruling to the South Carolina Supreme Court which reversed Judge Cooper's ruling. The court held that the Pawley Land Trust had "executed," and that the All Saints Church land had vested in the church corporation known as the Parish of All Saints and its successor, All Saints Parish, Waccamaw that had been formed in 1902.

However, the South Carolina Supreme Court also ruled that both TEC and the Diocese had given up any rights that they may have had in the All Saints Church property in 1903 when they executed a "quit-claim" deed to All Saints Parish, Waccamaw. To the dismay of the attorneys for TEC, the court ruled further that the Dennis Canon had no affect on the property of All Saints Church, nor did it have any affect on the property of *any* Episcopal Church in South Carolina.

TEC and a group of loyal Episcopalians filed a request for permission to appeal to the United States Supreme Court. The Diocese of South Carolina did not join in their request. For years, the Primates of the Global South had encouraged diocesan Bishop Ed Salmon and his successor, Bishop Mark Lawrence, to end the litigation with All Saints Church. The case was unique because the Diocese of South Carolina was orthodox, as was the leadership of All Saints Church. Therefore, two theologically conservative factions were suing each other, unlike the other TEC property litigation that involved orthodox parishes and liberal, revisionist bishops. The All Saints Church case was settled finally in early 2010, after ten years of contentious and very expensive litigation.

Having a state supreme court rule in favor of a local TEC congregation was nothing less than a miracle. Courts in Connecticut, Colorado, North Carolina, California, Florida, Texas, Georgia, and Virginia respectively, and the United States Supreme Court had ruled that property owned by Episcopal (and Presbyterian and Methodist) congregations was held "in trust" for the denomination. In those states, the courts ruled that local congregations that had withdrawn from the denomination had to turn their property over to the national churches even though, in most cases, the national churches had contributed little if anything financially to the purchase of the property.

<u>The Dennis Canon Does Not Create a Trust—It is a Legal Fiction</u>

For over a decade, Ross Lindsay, the Chancellor of All Saints Church, a trust lawyer and a canon lawyer, had maintained that the Dennis Canon (and similar canons in the Presbyterian and Methodist churches) did not create a trust in favor of the national church— that it was a "legal fiction." The Roman, English, and American common law were consistent that in order to create a trust, a "Grantor" (sometimes referred to as a "Settlor") first had to *own* property, and then *convey* that property to one or more trustees, who *held* the property for the exclusive benefit of a third party.

Percival and Anna Pawley met all of these requirements when they conveyed the All Saints Church property to the Pawley Land Trust in 1745. The Pawleys owned the 60 acres. They *transferred* title to the property to George Pawley and William Poole as trustees, and the trustees *held* the property for the benefit of the inhabitants of the Waccamaw Neck. Neither The Episcopal Church nor the Diocese of South Carolina *owned* any of the *All Saints Church* property, so they had no property to *convey* to a trust, nor could they legally name themselves as the beneficiaries of the trust, which is precisely what the "Dennis Canon" purported to do.

The Supreme Court of South Carolina was the first state Supreme Court to confirm what Ross Lindsay had been shouting from the rooftops to seemingly deaf ears since the All Saints Church property litigation began in 2000—that the Pawley Land Trust was a valid trust, and that the "Dennis Canon" was a "legal fiction." In their defense, the church lawyers who have defended the church property cases for the other theologically conservative Episcopal (and Presbyterian) congregations are not "trust lawyers" or "canon lawyers." These "litigators" have little if any knowledge and understanding of these complex areas of canon law, and very few Anglican canon lawyers exist in the United States to enlighten them.

The Centre for Law and Religion at Cardiff Law School in Cardiff, Wales is the only law school in the world that offers a Master of Laws (L.L.M.) in Anglican Canon law. Only four Americans have received their L.L.M.'s in Canon Law from Cardiff Law School, and only two of them are lawyers: Ross Lindsay and another attorney from Baton Rouge, Louisiana.

The All Saints Church Case Was Cited as Precedent by Other Breakaway Anglican Churches

The parishioners at All Saints Church had hoped that some of the other larger breakaway Anglican churches would prevail in the courts before it did, so that All Saints Church could rely upon their cases as precedent and not have to wage the expensive decade long court battle that it did. Instead, the All Saints Church case was the first major victory for a breakaway Anglican church. Therefore, the All Saints Church case was soon cited as precedent by several other breakaway Anglican churches whose legal battles were continuing.

In 2011, breakaway Anglican church property cases were on appeal to the Supreme Courts of Virginia, Georgia, Texas, and California; and the briefs filed by the attorneys in all of these cases cited the All Saints Church case as precedent. All Saints Church had lived into its Vision Statement. It had become a people who risk boldly in sharing the Full Counsel of God, bringing encouragement *to the Church and the World* [emphasis added].

The South Carolina Supreme Court Gave Bishop Lawrence the "Keys to the Kingdom"

The great news for the other theologically conservative Episcopal congregations in South Carolina was that the ruling of the South Carolina Supreme Court was not limited to the property of All Saints Church. The court not only ruled that The Episcopal Church had no interest in the property of All Saints Church, the court ruled also that the "Dennis Canon" had no validity in South Carolina. Therefore, the Dennis Canon did not apply to any of the property of any of the Episcopal churches in South Carolina.

This ruling effectively gave Mark Lawrence, the Bishop of the Diocese of South Carolina (Bishop Salmon's successor), the "keys to the Kingdom." After the Supreme Court ruling, Bishop Lawrence had the legal authority to move the entire Diocese of South Carolina, property and all, out of The Episcopal Church, when and if he chose to do so.

When he was being interviewed as a candidate for Bishop of the Diocese of South Carolina, Mark Lawrence was asked if he intended to take the Diocese of South Carolina out of TEC. Lawrence was then resident in the Diocese of San Jaoquin, California which was the second entire diocese to withdraw from TEC. Lawrence responded: "I will try as hard to keep the Diocese of South Carolina in TEC, as TEC tries to stay in the Anglican Communion." This poignant response demonstrated the intellect and the foresight of South Carolina's new bishop. After the ruling of the South Carolina Supreme Court in the All Saints case, the Diocese of South Carolina and its new bishop took center stage.

12

TEC AMENDED ITS DISCIPLINARY CANONS AND ALL EYES WERE ON THE DIOCESE OF SOUTH CAROLINA

The weapon that the revisionist bishops within TEC had used most frequently and effectively against the orthodox TEC priests and congregations was the TEC Disciplinary Canons. The first TEC *disciplinary canons* can be traced directly to the English disciplinary canons of 1603, with one exception. The English disciplinary canons provided for a sentence of *deprivation,* whereby a clergyman was deprived of his benefices and promotions (his support) but not the exercise of his ministerial functions. White and Dykman speculated that the American insistence upon the separation of church and state necessarily relegated matters of clergy support, and issues involving personal and real property, to the "civil courts."

The TEC canons that deal with clergy discipline are quite lengthy. Writing in 1930, Bishop E. L. Parsons described the disciplinary canons in this way:

> It has been remarked at times that anyone looking through the Constitution and Canons of the Episcopal Church might think that the chief work of the Church is that of putting bishops and presbyters [priests] on trial, so long and detailed are the articles dealing with the matter.

Although the TEC disciplinary canons were lengthy, P.M. Dawley wrote in 1955 that the canons were of "little general interest and of infrequent application." Dawley further described the "ecclesiastical courts" provided for in the canons as "vestigial remnants of the more elaborate ecclesiastical juridical system of the Middle Ages" noting that today the courts "have become internal tribunals, the function of which is restricted to *infrequent* trials of the clergy' [emphasis added]."

Much has changed in the judicatories of TEC in the 50 years since Dawley made these observations. Since 2000, the TEC disciplinary canons have been applied by revisionist bishops against orthodox priests in the Diocese of Southwest Florida, the Diocese of Los Angeles, the Diocese of Connecticut, the Diocese of Florida, the Diocese of Virginia, and against the orthodox Bishop of San Joaquin.

For example, on February 6, 2002, the Rt. Rev. John Lipscomb, Bishop of the Diocese of Southwest Florida, inhibited the Rev. Kevin Donlon of St. Mary's Parish, Tampa for "conduct unbecoming of a member of the clergy," despite the fact that he had no direct evidence to substantiate the claims. On April 22, 2003,

Bishop Lipscomb "deposed" Father Donlon *in absentia*, without a trial.

On August 19, 2004, Bishop Jon Bruno of the Diocese of Los Angeles inhibited four orthodox priests in Southern California, declaring that they had "abandoned the communion of this Church" after they had each sought alternative episcopal oversight from the Archbishop of Uganda, the Most Rev. Henry Luke Orombi. On March 29, 2005, the Rt. Rev. Andrew D. Smith of the Diocese of Connecticut notified six orthodox rectors in his diocese, who had expressed opposition to the consecration of Gene Robinson, that they had "abandoned the communion of this Church," a canonical offense for which they could be inhibited or deposed. On July 13, 2005, Bishop Smith actually inhibited one of the six rectors, the Rev. Mark Hansen of St. John's Church, Bristol.

On November 27, 2006, Bishop John Howard of Florida deposed six of the first seven North Florida priests who had sought alternative episcopal oversight with "abandoning communion with this Church." The Rev. Neil Lebhar, one of the priests who was deposed made the following comment:

> It is ironic that the charge brought against the seven priests is "abandonment of communion," since one of the major reasons that they felt they had no choice but to separate from the Episcopal Church was to stay in communion with the vast majority of the world's 80 million Anglicans who have condemned the Episcopal church USA's unbiblical actions. . . .
> By inhibiting me, I believe the Bishop and Standing Committee have effectively agreed that they are not in communion with Uganda, one of the largest provinces of the Anglican Communion.

Also, in 2006, TEC bishops of Los Angeles and San Diego, California, and Northern California charged Bishop John-David Schofield of San Joaquin with abandoning the communion, citing changes made to the diocesan constitution and canons at the 2005 diocesan convention. A TEC Title IV Review Committee later ruled that Bishop Schofield was not guilty.

Finally, on January 22, 2007, Bishop Peter Lee of the Diocese of Virginia became the latest TEC bishop to use the TEC disciplinary canons to inhibit orthodox priests in his diocese. Bishop Lee deposed 21 priests of breakaway parishes that had abandoned the Communion of the Episcopal Church and rejected its authority.

Canons 9 and 10: Abandonment of the Communion
Title IV, Canons 9 and 10 of the TEC *Canons* proscribe the juridical response that may be imposed if a bishop or priest abandons the communion of this Church. According to White and Dykman, these canons were adopted by the TEC General Convention of 1853 after Bishop Ives of North Carolina submitted himself to the Church of Rome. Therefore, several TEC orthodox bishops and priests have expressed surprise and outrage that the revisionist bishops would utilize these particular canons to depose their orthodox counterparts who had sought alternative episcopal oversight from other churches *within the wider Anglican Communion* all of whom were in communion with the See of Canterbury.

General Convention 2006 Prompts Amendments to Diocesan Canons
Following the 2006 TEC General Convention, two dioceses amended their *Constitutions and Canons*

to affirm their inclusion within the wider Anglican Communion and to ensure canonically that they could exit from TEC if it became necessary to do so in the near future. On October 20, 2006, the Diocese of Dallas in Convention amended the Preamble and Article I of its *Constitution*. The Preamble was amended to affirm that the Diocese was "a constituent member of the Anglican Communion—a Fellowship of those Dioceses, Provinces, and regional churches in communion with the See of Canterbury, upholding and propagating the historic Faith and Order as set forth in the *Book of Common Prayer*."

Article I of the *Constitution* was also amended to include the following language:

> The foregoing accession [to the TEC *Constitution and Canons*] is expressly premised on [TEC] remaining a full, constituent member of the Anglican Communion . . . . In the event such premise shall no longer be applicable . . . such accession may be revoked . . . . Moreover, the foregoing accession shall in no way be deemed to prevent or limit the Diocese from disassociating itself from any actions of the General Convention.

Finally, Canon 20 was amended to facilitate an "amicable conclusion" to "controversies between a Parish and the Diocese" if such occurred in the future.

The Diocese of San Joaquin was the second TEC diocese to amend its *Constitution and Canons* following the 2006 TEC General Convention. Prior to its convention, the diocese had posted thirteen proposed amendments to its *Constitution and Canons* which, if adopted, would have placed the diocese "in an ideal position to be part of any ecclesiastical structure that the Archbishop of Canterbury and Primates might design."

However, after last minute pleas from Presiding Bishop Jefferts Schori and assurances from Archbishop Gregory Venables of the Southern Cone that a new orthodox structure for the United States would be considered by the Primates at their February 2007 meeting in Tanzania, the delegates approved four amendments to its diocesan *Constitution and Canons*.

The first amendment to Article I of the San Joaquin *Constitution* permitted the diocese to unilaterally redefine its geographical boundaries. The second amendment changed Article II of its *Constitution* by deleting this sentence:

> The Church in the Diocese of San Joaquin accedes to The Constitution of the Episcopal Church of the United States of America.

and replaced it with the following:

> The Diocese of San Joaquin is constituted by the Faith, Order, and Practice of the One Holy Catholic, and Apostolic Church as received by the Anglican Communion. This church is a constituent member of the Anglican Communion and is in full communion with the See of Canterbury.

The third amendment approved by the San Joaquin delegates affirmed that the "ecclesiastical authority of the diocese is the bishop;" however, all references to "the National Canons" of TEC were deleted. Similarly, the fourth amendment deleted all references to "Protestant Episcopal'" from Article XII of its *Constitution*. The Rt. Rev. Mark Lawrence, the

Bishop of the Diocese of South Carolina came to South Carolina from the Diocese of San Joaquin. At its 2010 and 2011 diocesan conventions, the Diocese of South Carolina amended its canons precisely as the Diocese of San Joanquin had done three years earlier.

TEC Attempts to Amend its Disciplinary Canons to Include the Laity

While the TEC disciplinary canons gave the diocesan bishops unlitateral control and power over the priests of the dioceses, these canons did not give the bishops any control over the laity, nor did these canons give the Presiding Bishop of TEC any control or power over the diocesan bishops. TEC is a "fellowship" or "communion" of autonomous dioceses. Like the Archbishop of Canterbury, the Presiding Bishop of TEC is the "first among equals," and as such she convenes and presides over meetings of the House of Bishops, but she had no governing or disciplinary authority over the bishops. Therefore, soon after Jefferts Schori was elected Presiding Bishop, she and her Chancellor, David Booth Beers sought to rectify this situation.

Following its General Convention in 2006, TEC published proposed changes to the Title IV Disciplinary Canons. For the first time, the proposed canons gave the Presiding Bishop and the Diocesan Bishops disciplinary authority over the laity. Why would the Presiding Bishop want disciplinary authority over the laity?

In the case of All Saints Church and most of the other orthodox parishes that had severed their ties with TEC, the lay members of the Vestry, not the clergy, voted to amend their respective constitutions and canons and then voted to leave TEC. The Supreme Court of South Carolina ruled that All Saints Church could retain its property because it followed these steps. The Vestry and the members of the congregation amended their constitution and by-laws first, before voting to leave TEC. Jefferts Schori and Beers recognized this for what it was—a hole in the Dennis Canon dike, a hole that would grow larger and larger if the lay members of the Vestries of other orthodox parishes took the same steps that All Saints Church had.

After much wailing and gnashing of teeth on the part of the laity, even revisionist lay persons, and a barrage of negative press, TEC reluctantly withdrew its proposed canon that would have given the Presiding Bishop and the diocesan bishops control over the laity. However, TEC pressed on with the other proposed amendments that bolstered the authority of the Presiding Bishop over TEC bishops and priests.

TEC Amended Its Disciplinary Canons at its 2009 General Convention

TEC amended Title IV of its canon law, the disciplinary canons, at its 2009 General Convention. The amendment granted specific authority to the Presiding Bishop to intervene in matters involving local parishes. However, the effective date of the amendment was delayed until July 1, 2011.

In response to the TEC amendments, the Diocese of South Carolina amended its canons at its Diocesan Conventions in 2010 and 2011 in order to assert its "legal autonomy" from The Episcopal Church while remaining "in fellowship" with The Episcopal Church. Typical church constitutions and canons contain "accession" clauses wherein the congregation or diocese "accedes" to the constitution and canons of the larger, national church.

Prior to withdrawing from TEC, a majority of the members of All Saints Church voted to amend its

Constitution and Canons to delete the "accession" clauses and all references to TEC in its corporate charter and by-laws. Since these amendments were proposed and adopted by a majority of the members in accordance with its by-laws and the law of South Carolina, the Supreme Court said that TEC had no claim on the All Saints Church property.

The Dennis Canon specified that all of property of Episcopal congregations was held in trust for TEC and the Dioceses, but neither the Dennis Canon nor any other provisions of the TEC Constitution and Canons prohibited a majority of the members of a TEC congregation from voting to leave TEC. Nor did the TEC Constitution or Canons prohibit a Diocesan Bishop or the majority of the delegates at a Diocesan Convention from voting to take the entire diocese out of TEC.

The ruling of the South Carolina Supreme Court had opened "Pandora's Box," and Jefferts Schori and David Beers were determined to put the lid back on it. The majority of the delegates to the TEC 2009 Convention amended the Title IV disciplinary canons precisely as Jefferts Schori and Beers had requested except for the provisions governing the laity that had been dropped.

The Diocese of South Carolina Responded

The South Carolina Supreme Court had given Mark Lawrence, the Bishop of the Episcopal Diocese of South Carolina, the keys to the Kingdom, and while he had no intention of taking the Diocese out of TEC at that time, he did not want to give up the right to do so in the future, if subsequent events forced him to do so.

Therefore, at its 2010 and 2011 Annual Conventions, Bishop Lawrence and the Standing Committee of the Diocese of South Carolina, proposed amendments to the diocesan canons to affirm that the Diocese of South

Carolina was an autonomous legal entity governed by its bishop and standing committee and "in fellowship" with the other dioceses of TEC. The "accession" clause was removed from the "canons" of the diocese, but not from its constitution.

Jefferts Schori and Beers were furious. They hired a South Carolina attorney (and former chancellor of the Diocese of South Carolina) to serve as independent counsel for TEC in South Carolina, since Beers was not licensed to practice law in South Carolina. Bishop Lawrence and his legal defense team sprang into action with a letter to Jefferts Schori and Beers demanding that they cease and desist from any legal actions in South Carolina since the TEC canons gave them no authority to do so. Many were surprised when Jefferts Schori and David Booth Beers did indeed cease and desist, for the time being. They had no choice because the new Title IV amendments were not effective until July 1, 2011.

As July 2011 approached, all eyes were on South Carolina. Many Episcopalians in South Carolina, both liberals and conservatives, sensed that the "saber-rattling" between Bishop Lawrence and Presiding Bishop Jefferts Schori would lead soon to a full-scale war of independence. The TEC Title IV amendments had a delayed effective date of July 1, 2011. Therefore, speculation was rampant that Presiding Bishop Jefferts Schori planned to depose Diocesan Bishop Mark Lawrence as soon as possible after July 1, 2011.

Soon the reporter from the *Wall Street Journal* would be calling again and asking a similar but different question: "Why South Carolina? Why Mark Lawrence?" To which someone might reply: "The first battle of the theological war between the breakaway Anglican churches and the revisionist TEC bishops occurred in

South Carolina. Why should not the last one also occur in South Carolina?"

If Mark Lawrence were able to lead the entire Diocese of South Carolina out of TEC unscathed, then the war would be over. The hole in the dike would quickly morph into open floodgates. The remaining theologically conservative churches in TEC would bolt for the door, and TEC would become a mere vestige of its former self, a dot on the historical landscape of the church in the United States and the wider Anglican Communion. 2011 would mark the end of the reign of terror of the revisionist bishops over the breakaway Anglican churches.

13

CONCLUSION

This book has traced the emergence of the break-away Anglican churches and the new religious movement that emanated therefrom. It has also examined the political and juridical contexts in which the breakaway Anglican churches and the movement emerged. However, according to the Rev. John Yates, the Rector of The Falls Church, Virginia, one of the oldest and largest of the breakaway Anglican churches, the core issue facing these breakaway Anglican churches and the movement was not political or juridical. It was purely theological.

According to Yates, "The American Episcopal Church no longer believed the historic, orthodox Christian faith common to all believers," and he cited five specific examples:

1. Episcopal revisionism has abandoned the fidelity of faith. The Hebrew scriptures linked matters of truth to a relationship with God.
2. Episcopal revisionism has negated the authority of faith. The "sola scriptura" (by the scriptures alone) doctrine of the Reformation church has been aban-

doned for the "sola cultura" (by the culture alone) way of the modern church.

3. Episcopal revisionism has severed the community of faith cutting itself off from the universal faith that has spanned centuries and continents.

4. Episcopal revisionism has destroyed the credibility of faith. There is little that is distinctively Christian left in the theology of some Episcopal leaders. It is no accident that orthodox churches are growing. . . . The prospect for The Episcopal Church, already evident in many dioceses, is inevitable withering and decline.

5. Episcopal revisionism has obliterated the very identity of the faith. When the great truths of the Bible and the creeds are abandoned, and there is no limit to what can be believed in their place, then the point is reached when there is little identifiably Christian in Episcopal revisionism.

Without question, the core issue for the breakaway Anglican churches was theological as Yates maintained, and for over ten years, godly leaders like Chuck Murphy and Bob Duncan had risked their positions, their power, their pensions, and their property in order to restore the faith that was given to the Saints.

However, those breakaway Anglican churches that had severed their ties with TEC soon found themselves in a "brave new world," one generally devoid of juridical authority and structure. Once the "faith" that was given to the Saints was restored, the "order" given to the Saints also needed to be restored.

The Rev. James E. Hampson, Jr., a retired TEC priest who attended St. Peter's Anglican Church in Tallahassee, Florida observed: "We need canons. Some breakaway Anglican churches are allowing their parishioners to hire and fire their rectors. Without canons, we invite trouble." Hampson suggested that the breakaway Anglican churches "turn the clock back" and adopt the TEC canons that existed prior to 1991, before the revisionist bishops gained control of TEC.

Bishop Chuck Murphy, the Chairman of The Anglican Mission, also acknowledged the need for a concise set of canons. However, Murphy added that the canons should be no more than twenty pages, unlike the TEC *Constitution and Canons* that have morphed into 253 pages over its two hundred year history. Others suggested that completely new canons be drafted that affirmed orthodoxy and incorporated the "Anglican Covenant" as proposed by *The Windsor Report.*

Part 1 of this book examined the emergence of the breakaway Anglican churches in their political contexts. Part 2 of this book examined the emergence of the breakaway Anglican churches in their juridical contexts. Appendix I contains a proposal by Emmanuel Kolini and Kevin Donlon that explains why the proposed "Anglican Covenant" is not sufficient to deal with an apostate church like TEC and why a "church council" is the only effective strategy for restoring the "faith" that was delivered to the Saints. Appendix II of this book contains a Model Constitution and Canons that can be adapted and adopted by breakaway Anglican churches in order to preserve "order" in their congregations.

Once the *faith* and the *order* are restored unto the church, it will flourish once again. The new reformation will be in full bloom. To God be the glory if this book assists in some small way in that process.

Calling for a Church Council– Primates, Structures, and Communion

A Draft Paper on Communion Structures by Emmanuel M. Kolini, Archbishop of the Anglican Church of Rwanda and Kevin F. Donlon, Canon for Ecclesiastical Affairs of the Anglican Mission in the Americas as Presented to the Delegates to the Fourth Global South Encounter in Singapore in April 2010

A Primer on Primatial Authority and Ecclesiastical Structures for the 21st Century

It is clear from a study of the canonical tradition on the topics of communion and mission that the Anglican Covenant lacks the significance and substance to unify Anglicanism and arbitrarily decides who is authentically Anglican. The Covenant is not the frame of reference for unity and probably cannot ever be. We should never lose sight that our tradition calls for the college of bishops in "Synod" to embody and act as the expression of the Church's unity. It is very significant, however, that whenever and wherever the federated view of "canonical subordinationism" triumphs, the idea of the catholic unity dissipates and, therefore, the concept of a college of bishops becomes dormant and ineffective.

To address this point there are three principal concerns that require further elucidation.

ELUCIDATION #1

Is there a precedent for the Primates to act according to biblical norms in accord with the General Canonical Tradition of the Church and in accordance with historic understanding of Communion in the undivided church? This question recognizes the challenge of understanding Primatial authority in its biblical and juridical sense.

ELUCIDATION #2

Is the Anglican Covenant adequate in discussion of Communion?

This question recognizes the challenge to maintain "*communio*" in tension with local autonomy in relation to Primatial authority.

ELUCIDATION #3

What responsibilities do the Primates have by virtue of their office and what power do they have to discharge those responsibilities?

The present Anglican Covenant raises these questions because this is as much a struggle of ecclesiology (order) as it is of doctrine (faith). Despite considerable progress toward convergence on many divisive issues, orthodox Anglicans are faced with pressing ecclesiological questions that may restrain authentic unity. These elucidations are deeply theological and frame perhaps what is the root issue in the present ecclesiastical crisis.

ELUCIDATION #1

Is there a precedent for the Primates to act according to biblical norms in accord with the General Canonical Tradition of the Church and in accordance with historic understanding of Communion in the undivided church?

A) The Biblical Context

Authority in the Church of God resides in the person of the glorified Jesus Christ, the witness of the Scriptures and of those to whom He entrusted it. The self emptying (kenosis) of God in Christ gave us a model of authority that is radically different from the authority of the rulers of this world who "lord it over the people". Christ's authority, on the contrary, was "to serve and to give his life as a ransom for many" (Mark 10: 42-44).

The authority he gave to the apostles consisted in healing all kinds of sickness, forgiving sins and announcing the good news of the kingdom of God (Luke 9: 1-2) as well as all power to build the Church and to guide it. Christ promised to them the continuing presence of the Holy Spirit who guides the Church to the fullness of truth.

Moreover, Paul indicates to the presbyters at Miletus (Acts 20: 28-30) that they have duties to safeguard God's flock and themselves from attack. The seriousness of this duty to watch and guard is indicated by its repetition (verses 28 and 31) and by the imagery of "fierce wolves" to describe false teachers, imagery that suggests both savagery and intense destructiveness. Primates are not relieved by their office of their presbyterial responsibilities, rather the contrary. A greater office suggests greater responsibility.

B) The Patristic Context

Jurisdiction can be generally understood *as the capacity of exercising authority* that is recognized by other Churches. This can be expressed in the following ways.

1. For a Primate as Metropolitan (and other bishops) to make the decisions required by his office.
2. For a synod or a council to make decisions in defining the faith of the Church and in establishing its discipline, in such a way that these decisions are binding for the local Churches concerned or even for the Church Catholic (e.g. the jurisdiction of an ecumenical council).
3. For a primate to represent a regional Church and to preside, in various ways, over synods and councils that make decisions for the good of the church on matters brought before them.

In the general tradition of the church, metropolitan archbishops or primates can, in discharging the duties of safeguarding the flock, call councils. The power to call councils is consonant with the duties set out in Acts 20, since such councils can by public declaration unite and protect God's flock against false teaching that may have arisen within the church.

Early councils dealing with urgent issues such as modalism, the christological controversies over the natures of Christ, and some of the phases of the Arian controversy should be seen in just this light, and they resulted not just in theological decisions, but sometimes in the deposition of offending parties. (For example, Nestorius in the christological controversy and Eusebius of Nicomedia at the end of the Council of Nicaea). Metropolitans acted to call councils as particular situations arose, because the rights and responsibilities they possessed called for it.

It is myopic understanding that this power to call councils on the part of metropolitans does not extend outside of their jurisdictions. Cyprian of Carthage acts extra-territorially in adjudicating on the Spanish bishops Basilides and Martial (Epistle 67). Cyril of Alexandria acts extra-territorially against another metropolitan, Nestorius, while Hilary of Poitiers even acted against his own metropolitan, Saturninus of Arles. All of these cases related to the deposition of bishops or metropolitans.

Therefore it can be said that jurisdiction is an aspect of the

- sacramental,
- pastoral
- teaching authority of the bishop

and it should not be dissociated from its spiritual roots as constituting a different power in imitation of secular authority. Canon 9 of the Council of Antioch captures this understanding and frames for the present application:

"It behooves the bishops in every province to acknowledge the bishop who presides in the metropolis, and who has to take thought for the whole province; because all men of business come together from every quarter to the metropolis. Wherefore it is decreed that he have precedence in rank, and that the other bishops

do nothing extraordinary without him, (according to the ancient canon that prevailed from [the times of] our Fathers) or such things only as pertain to their own particular parishes and the districts subject to them".

ELUCIDATION #2
Is the Anglican Covenant adequate in discussion of Communion?

This question recognizes the challenge to maintain "*communio*" in tension with local autonomy in relation to Primatial authority.

The role of the Primates in the Anglican Communion has developed in various and locally adapted ways. This is a problematic when one considers evolving into a Global Communion. This challenge was brought to the fore for the Primates of the Anglican Communion in the 1930 Lambeth Conference. The constitution adopted by that conference speaks of "the principle of the autonomy of *particular* churches" and later draws out the implications of autonomy in the event of disruption within the communion: the Lambeth Conference could not as such take disciplinary action because of autonomy. Instead autonomy means: Formal action would belong to the several Churches of the Anglican Communion *individually*.

While the Anglican Covenant rightly addresses the question of autonomy, it fails to articulate the Anglican understanding of Provincial autonomy expressed in the 1930 constitution and adopted by the Lambeth Conference. Provincial autonomy does not just deal with the freedom to develop individually, but the responsibilities and power individual Provinces and their Primates have to act to defend the faith once delivered and to affirm the notion of communio.

In the light of the failure it is important to realize this metropolitical authority and responsibility is distinct from that which is vested in the Anglican Communion's Primates' Meeting. Anglicanism as part of the catholic faith must seek to embrace an expression of *communion* that reflects the apostolic tradition both of Scripture and of conciliar teachings concerning the historic life and ministry of the church. How shall the Metropolitan Archbishops address the weakness of the Covenant and at the same time see that existing synodical and governing structures be renewed so that they may be truly conciliar and canonically effective implementing the discipline necessary for a common Anglican faith and order?

ELUCIDATION #3

What responsibilities do the Primates have by virtue of their office and what power do they have to discharge those responsibilities ?

The Primates by virtue of their historic office exercise authority on a local, regional or global level. As a group, they come together as college of Primates (as in the case of the Global South) for the purposes of common witness and common actions which are necessary for the common good of the faithful.

Each Primate is accustomed to exercising authority and jurisdiction on a local level, but with these actions now, the Primates need to *rediscover together* the normative principles and patterns of authority originating in the apostolic Church that is theirs. This is of crucial importance for the unity and communion of the Church.

The Primates as Metropolitans inherit by their role particular norms through positive law (*ius divinum positivum*- which derives from Christ's teachings and Divine Revelation), natural law (*ius divinum naturale*

- which is the given order deduced rationally), as well as human law (*ius humanum* - often established as a result of custom).

Despite the norms of the canonical tradition, there have been moments in the life of the community of faith when the need for exceptions (canonically known as dispensations) to what is considered the common order occurs. The criteria for such action in the ordering of the church are as follows:

1. The cause of the action must be an extraordinary circumstance that absolutely necessitates the ecclesial action;
2. The action is an exception through dispensation and not setting a precedent ; The reason for the action must be for the benefit of the wider church; and the ecclesial communion must not be diminished as a result.

CONCLUSIONS

A further governing principle for Primates/Metropolitans is

- that authentic catholicity must truly manifest itself in such action to effect communion with the other Churches that confess the same apostolic faith and share the same basic ecclesial structure,
- that the Primates have a continuing duty to safeguard God's flock in the present crisis and corresponding powers to discharge that duty.

THEREFORE In seeking to accomplish these governing principles the Anglican Covenant **does indeed possess an ecclesial deficit**.

- The Covenant needs a reconsideration of its concept of Provincial autonomy to reflect a richer understanding of comunio, which is rooted in the understanding and expression of the undivided church.

Therefore it is incumbent upon the Primates to assume the full measure of their metropolitical authority to effect communion for the good of Christ's Church through historic conciliar and canonical structures by calling a "church council to effectively resolve the controversy between the Global South Primates and the apostate Episcopal Church in the United States and the Anglican Church of Canada.

Appendix II

A Model Constitution and Canons for The Breakaway Anglican Churches

Sources, Assumptions, and Methodology

In developing this Model Constitution and Canons for the Breakaway Anglican Churches, the following sources were relied upon:

1. Responses to a survey of two hundred twenty-one priests of breakaway Anglican churches
2. The 39 Articles of Religion
3. The *Book of Common Prayer and Ordinal, 1662*
4. The Chicago-Lambeth Quadrilateral, 1886/1888
5. Lambeth Conference 1998: Resolution I.10 Human Sexuality Lambeth Conference 1998: Resolution III.2 The unity of the Anglican Communion
6. The Principles of Canon Law Common to the Churches of the Anglican Communion [PCLAC]
7. Solemn Declaration of Principles and the By-Laws of the Anglican Mission in the Americas

8. *Constitutions and Canons* of The Episcopal Church: 1789-1979
9. *Constitutions and Canons* of the following Global South Provinces: Rwanda, Uganda, Nigeria
10. *Constitutions and Canons* of the following orthodox TEC dioceses: Albany, Central Florida, Dallas, Fort Worth, Pittsburgh, Quincy, Rio Grande, San Joaquin, South Carolina, Springfield
11. *The Virginia Report* and *The Windsor Report*

The following assumptions were made in drafting the Model Constitution and Canons:

1. This Model Constitution and Canons will be adopted by a regional judicatory whether it be a diocese, network, or affinity group of local congregations that are supervised by at least one bishop.
2. Inclusion in the Anglican Communion and being in communion with the See of Canterbury will be affirmed along with the interdependence and the autonomy of the churches.
3. Orthodoxy will be affirmed by specific references to the supreme authority of Holy Scripture; the three Ecumenical Creeds; the first seven Ecumenical Councils; the Book of Common Prayer and Ordinal, 1662; the 39 Articles of Religion, and the Lambeth Quadrilateral, 1888.
4. Where appropriate, the "principles of canon law" identified by the Network of Anglican Legal Advisers will be included in the Model Constitution and Canons.
5. The TEC "Dennis Canon" will be intentionally excluded; however, other historic canons concerning church property will be included.
6. Where appropriate, the civil law principles that are utilized to achieve equity and fairness will be incor-

porated into the canons, especially in the disciplinary canons.

7. The length of the Model Constitution and Canons will be no more than twenty pages.

The methodology for drafting the Model Constitution and Canons was three-fold. First, an attempt was made to incorporate as many of the 100 "Principles of Canon Law Common to the Churches of the Anglican Communion" (as identified by the Network of Anglican Legal Advisers) into the Model. Second, the TEC Canons were used to supplement the other canons, especially the disciplinary canons. Third, and finally, additional provisions were adapted from the Solemn Declaration of Principles of the Anglican Mission and from several Constitutions and Canons of the orthodox TEC dioceses within the Network. The original intention had been to make extensive use of the Constitutions and Canons of those Global South churches that had offered alternative episcopal oversight to the break-away churches; however, the adaptation of the 100 principles, the *ius commune* of the Anglican Communion, eliminated the need for singling out the Constitutions and Canons of the Global South churches.

A Model Constitution and Canons for the Breakaway Anglican Churches

The following model contains a Preamble, a Constitution, and a set of Canons. The Model Constitution contains mostly broad principles of canon law. According to the Network of Anglican Legal Advisers:

A principle of canon law is a foundational proposition or maxim of general applicability which has a strong dimension of weight, is induced from the similarities of the legal system of churches, derives from the canonical tradition or other practices of the church, expresses a basic theological truth or ethical value, and is about, is implicit in, or underlies canon law.

Since the Model Constitution contains mostly "principles of canon law," few, if any, modifications should be required prior to its adoption by regional judicatories or local congregations. The Model Canons, on the other hand, deal with more specific areas of ministry and discipline. Therefore, more substantial modifications to the Model Canons will likely be made in order to accommodate local circumstances.

The insights gained from the surveys were combined with other classical sources of canon law in order to a present a Model Constitution and Canons for the governance of the Breakaway Anglican Churches until more definitive provincial and regional constitutions and canons are adopted. Additional canons will likely be made.

Canons will likely be made in order to accommodate local circumstances.

In the Model Constitution and Canons, "Parish" signifies the most localized ecclesiastical unit and is sometimes referred to as the "local congregation." "Central church assembly" means the central legislative assembly of the church which is sometimes referred to as the Convention or Synod.

Critics will consider the Model Constitution and Canons that follows too simplistic. When compared to the 253 pages that presently comprise the TEC Constitution and Canons, the Model does appear simplistic. However, the position of the draftsman was that it was better to begin with a simple, straightforward document that could be modified to suit local circumstances, than to begin with a more complex document that would need to be simplified to in order to be understood by the typical clergy and lay persons within the breakaway churches. One should also recall that TEC adopted only seventeen canons when it was established. The following model contains 28 canons.

PREAMBLE

We, the Clergy and Laity of this church, a constituent member of the Anglican Communion and in communion with the See of Canterbury, intend to uphold and propagate the historic Faith and Order received by the one, holy, catholic, and apostolic church. In doing so, we acknowledge and affirm that the canon law of this church exists to serve the church: by providing order, by facilitating communion among the faithful, by putting Christian values into action, and by helping to avoid and resolve all conflicts in a fair and equitable manner. In acknowledgment and affirmation of these truths, we adopt this Constitution and these Canons this _____ day of _____, 201__.

THE CONSTITUTION

Article I.   The Anglican Communion
1. This church shall be in full communion with the See of Canterbury and all churches, provinces, dioceses, and other regional and local judicatories within the Anglican Communion that uphold and propagate the historic faith and order as expressed in the Scriptures, the Ecumenical Creeds, and the Book of Common Prayer and Ordinal, 1662.
2. This church acknowledges that all churches within the Anglican Communion are juridically autonomous but collegially interdependent.
3. This church specifically affirms the findings of the Lambeth Commission as expressed in *The Windsor Report* including the concept of an "Anglican Covenant." When finalized and adopted, the Anglican Covenant shall be attached to this Constitution as an Appendix, and its provisions shall be incorporated herein by reference.

Article II.   Ecclesiastical Governance
1. This church is an autonomous unit of ecclesiastical jurisdiction with a central legislative assembly (or convention) that shall be described more fully in its Canons.
2. The Ecclesiastical Authority of this church shall be the Bishop.
3. A Standing Committee (or Council of Advice) made up of four Clergy and four Lay persons shall provide advice and counsel to the Bishop and shall serve as the Ecclesiastical

Authority in the absence of a Bishop. The members of the Standing Committee (or Council of Advice) shall be elected by a majority vote of delegates entitled to vote at the annual meeting of the legislative body, and the members shall serve staggered three (3) year terms.

4. This church shall comply with the civil law of the state in which it is located and with the laws of the United States.

5. This Model Constitution and Canons hereby specifically incorporates by reference the Federal Rules of Civil Procedure, the Federal Rules of Evidence, and confers upon the Clergy and Lay persons all rights conferred upon them by the United States Constitution including but not limited to the rights to: a speedy trial, reasonable notice of proceedings, be represented by independent counsel, the presumption of innocence, and the right to appeal to a higher ecclesiastical or civil tribunal as prescribed in the Canons.

6. In addition to the Clergy, duly qualified Lay persons shall be eligible to serve in all levels of the government of this church, and neither this Constitution nor any Canon shall be adopted, repealed or amended without the approval of two-thirds (2/3) of both the Clergy and Lay delegates of the legislative body.

7. Ecclesiastical disputes shall be resolved amicably and equitably. The ecclesiastical and civil courts shall be remedies of last resort.

Article III. Ministry

1. This church recognizes the threefold ministry of bishops, priests, and deacons.
2. Bishops shall govern, teach, and minister. The priests shall assist the bishops in the care of souls, and deacons shall assist both the bishops and the priests. Parish priests and deacons exercise ministry under the general authority, oversight, and pastoral direction of their bishop.
3. All clergy shall conduct their ministry so as to: (a) give glory to God; (b) advance the Gospel; (c) maintain peace and unity within the church; (d) nurture, challenge, and strengthen their fellow ministers, the faithful, and the lost; and (e) share faith, hope, and the love of Christ with all people.

Article IV. Membership

1. Membership in this church shall be dependent upon a profession of faith, adherence to the doctrines of the church, and submission to this Constitution and Canons.
2. The names of all members shall be entered into a parish register.

Article V. Doctrine

1. The Holy Scriptures, the sixty-six books of the Old and New Testaments, shall be the supreme doctrinal authority in this church. Holy Scripture is the Word of God written and contains all things necessary for salvation.
2. The Book of Common Prayer and the Ordinal, 1662 shall also have doctrinal authority in this church. Revisions of the Book of

Common Prayer and alternative rites may be utilized as long as they are consistent with the doctrinal norms and formularies contained in the 1662 Book of Common Prayer; the three Ecumenical Creeds: the Nicene Creed, the Apostles Creed, and Athanasius' Creed; the dogmatic definitions of the first seven Ecumenical Councils, the 39 Articles of Religion, and the Lambeth Quadrilateral, 1888.

Article VI. Church Property
1. Legal title to all property utilized by local congregations shall be indefeasibly vested in the local congregation, or in a corporation owned and controlled by the local congregation, or in one or more trustees of a charitable land trust that are appointed or elected by the local congregation and hold the local church property in trust for the benefit of the local congregation.
2. Notwithstanding the provisions of Paragraph 1, no Vestry, officers of the Corporation, Trustees, or other body authorized by any State to hold property for the local congregation shall alienate any consecrated Church or Chapel which has been used for Divine Service without the previous consent of the Bishop, or in the Bishop's absence, the consent of the Standing Committee (or Council of Advice). Such consent shall not be unreasonably withheld.
3. The responsibility for the maintenance and management of all local church property shall be exercised by the Vestry (or Parish

Council) of the local congregation as further prescribed in the Canons.

4. All local congregations shall submit to their bishop, or his designee, annually an audited financial statement for the local congregation prepared by an independent certified public accountant.

Article VII. Dissolution

This Constitution may be amended by the affirmative vote of two-thirds (2/3) of those clergy and lay delegates that have the authority to vote at two successive annual meetings of the legislative body (conventions) or other special meetings called for that purpose.

If this church or any legal entity affiliated with this church shall be dissolved, no part of its assets shall inure to the benefit of the members or any other individuals. Rather, all of the church's assets, after the payment of its liabilities, shall be distributed to one or more other churches in communion with the See of Canterbury or alternatively to one or more orthodox Anglican missions organizations that have qualified for tax exempt status under Section 501(c)(3) of the Internal Revenue Code.

THE CANONS

Title I. Ecclesiastical Governance

1. Every Rector of a local congregation or (Vicar of a Mission) shall record in a Parish Register all baptisms, confirmations, marriages, burials, and the names of all members of the Parish (or local congregation).

2. A report of every Parish (or local congregation) of this church shall be prepared annually for the year ended December 31 and shall be submitted to the Bishop, or his designee, by March 1 of the following year. This report shall include a summary of the number of baptisms, confirmations, marriages, and burials during the year; the total number of baptized members; the total number of communicants; and a summary of the receipts and disbursements of the parish. In addition, an audited financial statement for the Parish (or local congregation) for its year ended December 31 shall be prepared by an independent certified public accountant. The audited financial statement shall be submitted to the Bishop, or his designee, by October 1 of the following year.

3. Every parish or local congregation shall hold an Annual Meeting not later than the last day of February each year. Confirmed persons in good standing and at least eighteen (18) years of age shall be qualified to vote at such meetings. A Special Meeting of the Parish may be called by the Rector and Wardens or by not less than thirty (30) members of the Parish (or local congregation). The Members

shall be given at least ten (10) days written notice all Annual and Special Meetings of the Parish (or congregation).

4. Every parish or local congregation shall elect members of the Vestry (or Parish Council) at its Annual Meeting, along with delegates to the central legislative assembly. The Vestry shall be composed of two Wardens and not less than three (3) nor more than ten (10) other persons who shall serve staggered three (3) year terms. Every local congregation shall elect at least one (1) delegate to the central legislative assembly. Provided however, that those local congregations that have average Sunday attendance in excess of one hundred (100) shall be entitled to elect additional delegates as provided below:

Average Sunday Attendance	Number of Delegates
1-100	1
100-200	2
201-400	3
401-600	4
600-or more	5

All members of the Vestry and delegates to the central assembly shall be "communicants" of this church. A 'communicant' shall be a person who, during the preceding twelve months, has been faithful in corporate worship and has contributed his or her time, talents, and financial resources toward the work and mission of the parish (or local congregation).

5. The Vestry of the Parish (or local congregation) shall: (a) manage the temporal affairs of the Parish (or local congregation; (b) elect and call a Rector (with the consent of the Bishop) and provide for the Rector's support; and (c) prepare annual budgets for adoption by the members of the congregation at the annual meeting of the Parish (or local congregation).

6. The Rector shall serve as President of the Vestry (or Parish Council) but may only vote in the event of a tie. The Rector shall provide the spiritual oversight of the Parish, and he or she shall at all times be entitled to the use and control of all church buildings and the contents thereof.

7. The Rector may not resign without the consent of the Vestry, and the Rector may not be removed without the consent of the Bishop or Standing Committee.

Title II. Ministry

1. All clergy and candidates for Holy Orders in this church shall annually subscribe to and affirm the doctrinal authority of this church by making the following oath: 'I do believe the Holy Scriptures of the Old and New Testaments to be the Word of God written and to contain all things necessary for salvation. I further affirm the catholic creeds, the dogmatic definitions of the General Councils of the undivided Church, the Book of Common Prayer and the Ordinal, 1662, the 39 Articles of Religion of the Church of England in their literal and grammatical sense, and the

Lambeth Quadrilateral of 1888; and I consider myself bound to teach nothing contrary thereto. Therefore, I do solemnly agree to conform to the Doctrines, Discipline, and Worship of this church.'

2. Christian initiation is effected by the ritual sequence of baptism, confirmation, and Holy Communion.

3. Baptism is a sign of regeneration or new birth by which those who receive it are incorporated into the church universal.

4. Baptism is administered with water by way of pouring, sprinkling, immersion, or submersion accompanied by the words: "I baptize you in the name of the Father, of the Son, and of the Holy Spirit."

5. Only baptized persons who have attained the age of discretion may be confirmed.

6. Confirmation is a rite by which baptized persons make a profession of faith and a mature expression or reaffirmation of their commitment to Christ made at baptism.

7. Confirmation shall be effected by episcopal laying on of hands and an invocation of the Holy Spirit to strengthen the candidate in Christian life.

8. Holy Communion (or the Eucharist) is a sacrament instituted by Christ, is the central act of worship, and shall be celebrated by every Parish (or local congregation) during at least one Sunday service each week.

9. This church upholds the faithfulness in marriage between one man and one woman in an exclusive lifelong union. In this church, "Holy Matrimony" and "marriage" shall mean the

exclusive physical and spiritual union of one man and one woman. The blessing of sexual relationships between persons of the same sex is prohibited.

Title III. Ecclesiastical Discipline
1. A Bishop, Priest, or Deacon of this church shall be liable for Presentment and Trial for the following offenses: (a) teaching publicly any doctrine contrary to that held by this church, (b) violating his or her Ordination vows, (c) violating any provision of the Constitution and Canons of this church.
2. Allegations of wrongdoing on the part of a Bishop, Priest, or Deacon shall be made in writing to the Standing Committee (or Council of Advice) of this church. A majority vote of the members of Standing Committee (or Council of Advice) is required for a Presentment.
3. If a Presentment if issued, an Ecclesiastical Trial Court composed of three members of the Clergy and three Lay Persons shall issue written notice of the time and place of the commencement of a Trial not less than thirty (30) days prior to its commencement. Provided however, the accused may waive such notice in order to expedite to the proceedings.
4. The accused shall: (a) be presumed innocent until found guilty; (b) have the opportunity to be heard in person; and (c) may be represented by counsel of his or her own choosing. The Chancellor, or church attorney, shall appear on behalf of the Standing Committee.

5. The accused may submit voluntarily to discipline of the church at any time prior to Judgment being rendered by the Ecclesiastical Trial Court or Civil Court.
6. The affirmative vote of two-thirds (2/3) of the members of the Ecclesiastical Trial Court shall be required for a Judgment to be rendered.
7. Any Judgment of the Ecclesiastical Trial Court may be appealed to a Court of Review which shall be composed of two bishops and two lay persons elected by a majority of the clergy and lay delegates to the annual legislative assembly.
8. The Ecclesiastical Trial Court may impose such Sentence as a majority its Members deem necessary and appropriate after considering all of the facts and circumstances of the case.
9. Nothing in these Canons shall prevent an accused from pursuing any remedies that may be available to him or her in any Federal or State tribunal, or from exercising any rights that he or she is guaranteed by the Constitution of the United States and of the laws of the state in which he or she resides.
10. To the extent possible, the Federal Rules of Civil Procedure including but not limited to the Federal Rules of Evidence shall be applied in all Ecclesiastical Courts of this church.

Title IV. Amendment and Repeal

No new Canon shall be adopted nor other Canon amended or repealed without the consent of two-thirds (2/3) of both the Clergy and Lay delegates eligible to vote at the annual legislative assembly (or convention) where the action is proposed. Any proposed amendment shall be submitted in writing to the delegates at least thirty (30) days prior to the meeting of the annual legislative assembly.

BIBLIOGRAPHY

Constitutions and Canons Reviewed

Provinces:
The Church of England
The Episcopal Church of the United States
The Church of Nigeria
The Church of Uganda
The Anglican Church of Rwanda

Orthodox Dioceses within TEC:
The Diocese of Albany
The Diocese of Central Florida
The Diocese of Dallas
The Diocese of Fort Worth
The Diocese of Pittsburgh
The Diocese of Rio Grande
The Diocese of San Joaquin
The Diocese of South Carolina
The Diocese of Springfield

Other Sources
ACNS 2050, "Report on Singapore Consecrations,'"
    February 24, 2000.
ACNS 2659, "Mixed Feelings as First Openly Gay
    Bishop Consecrated," November 3, 2003.

ACNS 3703, "Anglican provinces declare 'broken' and 'impaired' communion with ECUSA," December 9, 2003.

ACNS 3829, "Statement of the Global South Primates," May 19, 2004.

ACNS 3873, "Statement from the Archbishop of the Church of the Province of Uganda," August 23, 2004.

ACNS 4162, "ECUSA General Convention: Crowded hearing spotlights Windsor Report response", Anglican News Service, No 4162, June 16 2006.

ACNS 4193, "Global South Primates Meeting - Kigali Communiqué," September 22, 2006.

ACNS 4229, "Response from the Secretary General of the Anglican Communion Re: CANA," December 15, 2006.

ACNS 4235, Lambeth, "Archbishop of Canterbury announces Covenant Design Group," January 9, 2007.

ACNS LC 013, "Statement by the Archbishop for Armagh, The Most Reverend Robin Eames," July 18, 1998.

ACNS LC 094, "Lambeth takes conservative stance on Human Sexuality," August 5, 1998.

"A Covenant for the Church of England," December 12, 2006, accessed January 13, 2007, www.anglican-mainstream.net/?p=1034.

"A Pastoral Letter from the Moderator of the Anglican Communion Network," *Anglican Communion Network,* June 23, 2006.

"'A December 1999 report of a visit made to ECUSA at the invitation of the Presiding Bishop the Most Reverend Frank Griswold," accessed April 29, 2006, http://www.episcopalian.org/cclec/letter-december1999.htm.

"A Letter to Archbishop of Canterbury from Archbishops Tay and Kolini," January 30, 2000, http://www. episcopalian.org/cclec/letter-tay-kolini.htm, accessed April 29, 2006.

Barnum, Thaddeus, *Never Silent* (Colorado Springs, CO: Eleison Publishing, 2008).

"Bishop Duncan Testifies on ECUSA's Response to *Windsor Report,*" *Anglican Communion Network,* June 15, 2006. accessed June 15, 2006, http://www.acn-us.org/archive/2006/06/bishop-duncan-testifies-on-ecusas-response-to-the-windsor-report.html.

"Bishop Lee Inhibits 21 Priests," *The Living Church Foundation,* January 23, 2007.

"Bishop Spong Delivers a Fiery Farewell," *Christian Century,* February 17, 1999.

"Bishops Give Notice on Property," *The Living Church Foundation,* April 21, 2006.

Book of Order: The Constitution of the Presbyterian Church (U.S.A.), Part II, *2005/2007* (Louisville, KY: Office of the General Assembly, 2005)

Boorstein, M. and Salmon, J., "Episcopal Diocese Files Lawsuit Claiming Virginia Church Property," *Washington Post,* February 1, 2007, B04.

Brierly, Peter, *Religious Trends 5: UK Christian Handbook* (London, UK: Christian Research, 2005/2006).

Brumley, J., "Episcopal bishop revokes 6 priests," *The Florida Times-Union,* Jacksonville, Florida, December 9, 2006.

Burke, D., "Episcopal division widens in Virginia," *The Christian Century,* January 9, 2007, 11.

"Christ Church Takes Major Steps Toward its Mission," September 15, 2006, http://www.christchurchplano.

org/documents/06_0915_roseberry.html, accessed December 11, 2006.

"Costly Losses in Virginia," *The Living Church,* January 14, 2007, 12.

Dawley, P.M., *The Episcopal Church and Its Work* (Greenwich, CT: Seabury Press, 1955).

Doe, N., *Canon Law in the Anglican Communion* (Oxford, UK: Clarendon Press, 1998).

Doe, N., "Canon Law and Communion," *Ecclesiastical Law Journal,* 2002, 6(30):241-263.

Doe, N., "Common Law of the Anglican Communion," *Ecclesiastical Law Journal,* 2003, 7(32): 4-16.

Doe, N., "The Anglican Covenant Debate," a paper presented to canon law students at Cardiff Law School, July 11, 2006, 1.

Doe, N., "The Anglican Covenant Proposed by the Lambeth Commission," *Ecclesiastical Law Journal,* 2005, 8(37): 147-161.

Eames, R., *The Lambeth Commission on Communion: The Windsor Report:2004* (London, UK, Anglican Communion Office, 2004).

"Eight Virginia Parishes Vote to Leave Diocese," *The Living Church,* January 7, 2007, 20-21.

"Episcopal Church chided but not sanctioned," *Christian Century,* November 2, 2004, 10.

Evans, S., "Crisis, What Crisis?", http://www.episcopalian.org/cclec/paper-crisis.htm, February 10, 2000, accessed August 21, 2004.

"Falls Church, Truro Vestries Vote for Disaffiliation," *The Living Church,* 10 December 2006, 5.

Finke, R. and Stark, R., *The Churching of America: 1776-1990* (New Brunswick, NJ: Rutgers University Press, 1992).

"Furious Akinola Slams Report," *Church Times,* October 24, 2004.

"Gay Priest Rejects Bishop Post," *BBC News,* July 6, 2003, accessed August 23, 2004, http://news. bbc.co.uk/1/hi/uk/3049082.htm.

Grossman, C., "Female Bishop's Election Could Split Anglicans," *USA Today,* June 20, 2006, 6D.

Hadaway, C. Kirk and Marler, Penny, 'Propagation, Proselytization, and Retention: Interpreting the Growth, Decline, and Distribution of Religious Populations', A paper presented at the Society for the Scientific Study of Religion Annual Meeting held in Portland, Oregon on October 20, 2006.

Hadden, J, *The Gathering Storm in the Churches* (Garden City, NY: Doubleday, 1970).

Hill, M., *Ecclesiastical Law, Second Edition* (Oxford, UK: Oxford University Press, 2001).

Holmes, David, L., *A Brief History of the Episcopal Church* (Harrisburg, PA: Trinity Press, 1993).

Jenkins, P., *The Next Christendom* (Oxford, UK: Oxford University Press, 2002).

Journals of the General Convention of the Protestant Episcopal Church: 1904, 1907, 1979, 1982, 1985.

Lebhar, N., "Inhibited North Florida Priests Will Continue Their Ministries", Anglican Alliance of North Florida, January 12, 2006, 1.

Levin, J., "Anglicans urge disgruntled Episcopalians to join them," *The Pittsburgh Post-Gazette,* Vol. 79, No. 103, November 12, 2005, A-1.

Lindner, E., (ed.), *Yearbook of American & Canadian Churches: 1952, 1977, 2001, 2002, 2003, 2004, 2005, 2006 Editions* (Nashville, TN: Abingdon Press, 1952-2006).

Lindner, E., (ed.), *Yearbook of American & Canadian Churches: Historic Archive CD,* (Nashville, TN: Abingdon Press, 2005).

Lindsay, R., *Building a Church to Last: The Miracle in Pawleys* (Orlando, FL: Xulon Press, 2011).

McCaughan, P., "From Columbus: Episcopal Church Elects First Woman Presiding Bishop," *Episcopal News Service,* June 18, 2006, www.episcopalchurch.org/3577_76174_ENG_HTM.htm, accessed June 25, 2006.

Morrisey, F., "Canon Law Meets Civil Law," *Studia Canonica,* 32 (1988) 186-194.

Newman, A. and Stowe, S., "Connecticut Episcopalians Defy Bishop Over Gay Issues," *New York Times,* April 14, 2005.

Noyes, J., "Bishop Issues Statement to the Faithful Throughout the World," *Anglican Communion News-U.S.,* 21 June 2006, www.acn-us.org, accessed June 25, 2006.

Nunley, J., "Bishop Bruno Inhibits Breakaway Los Angeles Episcopal Priests," *Episcopal News Service,* August 19, 2004.

Parsons, E. L., "The Anglican Communion: USA" in *Episcopacy Ancient and Modern,* Jenkins and Mackenzie, (eds.) (London, UK: S.P.C.K., 1930) 170.

Prichard, Robert, *A History of the Episcopal Church* (Harrisburg, PA: Moorehouse Publishing, 1999).

"Province of South East Asia Breaks Communion with ECUSA," *Anglican Media Sydney,* December 3, 2003.

Restatement of the Law Third: Trusts, Vol. 2, Sec. 63 (New York, NY: The American Law Institute, 2003).

Roseberry, D., "Christ Church Affiliates with AMiA," January 26, 2007, accessed January 27, 2007, www.christchurchplano.org/amia.

Rosenthal, J., "Encounter in the South," *Anglican Communion News Service* (London, UK: March 1,1997).

Rucyahana, John, *The Bishop of Rwanda* (Nashville, TN: Thomas Nelson, 2007).

"San Joaquin Paves the Way for an Exit," *The Living Church,* December 24, 2006, 5.

Schjonberg, Mary Frances., "'San Joaquin Diocese to Consider Constitutional Amendments Severing Relationship with The Episcopal Church," *The Episcopal News Service*, October 2, 2006.

Schjonberg, Mary Frances, "Virginia leadership declares church property 'abandoned'", *Episcopal News Service*, January 18, 2007.

Sengupta, S. and Rohter L., "Where Faith Grows," *The New York Times,* CL III: 52, 636 (October 14, 2003) 1-A.

Shiflett, D., *Exodus, Why Americans are Fleeing Liberal Churches* (New York, NY: Penguin Group, 2005) 24-42.

Solheim, J., "Amid cheers and protests, Robinson consecrated in Diocese of New Hampshire," *Episcopal News Service,* November 2 2004.

Stevick, D., *Canon Law, A Handbook* (New York, NY: The Seabury Press, 1965).

"Temporary Property Agreement Reached in Diocese of Olympia," *The Living Church,* January 7, 2007, 21.

The Book of Discipline of the United Methodist Church: 2004 (Nashville, TN: The United Methodist Publishing House, 2004).

The Church of Nigeria, Anglican Communion, June 28, 2006, accessed on December 11, 2006, *http:// www.anglican-nig.org/bshpelects_jun2006.htm.*

The Lambeth Commission on Communion: The Windsor Report (London, UK:

The Anglican Communion Office, 2004).

"The Year in Review: 2004," *The Living Church,* December 26, 2004, 10-11.

"The Year in Review: 2006," *The Living Church,* December 28, 2004, 13-15.

Virtue, D., "Bishop Howe agrees to property settlement with Oviedo parish," *VirtueOnline,* http://listserv. episcopalian.org/wa.exe?A2=ind0512a&L=v irtueonline&T=0&P=346, 7 December 2005, accessed January 6, 2005.

"What Happened at the Primates Meeting?," *Anglican Communion News Service,ACNS 3635, ACO,* October 17, 2003.

White, E.A., *Constitution and Canons for the Government of the Protestant Episcopal Church Adopted in General Conventions 1789-1922* (New York, NY: Edwin S. Gorham, 1924).

White, E. and Dykman, J., *Annotated Constitution and Canons for the Government of the Protestant Episcopal Church in the United States of America otherwise known as The Episcopal Church* (New York, NY: Church Publishing, 1981).

Willard, Mary Weeks, *Emmanuel Kolini: The Unlikely Bishop of Rwanda* (Colorado Springs, CO: Authentic Publishing, 2008).

Wright, T., "A Confused Covenant: Initial Comments on 'A Covenant for the Church of England'" issued by Paul Perkin, Chris Sugden, and others, December 14, 2006.

Yates, J. and Guiness, O., "Why We Left the Episcopal Church," *The Washington Post,* January 8, 2007, A15.

Zeiger, H., "Episcopalians Pass Compromise Resolution Calling for Restraint," *VirtueOnline,* June 21, 2006, accessed June 23, 2006.

CPSIA information can be obtained at www.ICGtesting.com
Printed in the USA
BVOW04s1726300716

457024BV00001B/22/P